Sustaining Black Music and Culture during COVID-19

Sustaining Black Music and Culture during COVID-19

#Verzuz and Club Quarantine

Edited by
Niya Pickett Miller

LEXINGTON BOOKS
Lanham • Boulder • New York • London

Published by Lexington Books
An imprint of The Rowman & Littlefield Publishing Group, Inc.
4501 Forbes Boulevard, Suite 200, Lanham, Maryland 20706
www.rowman.com

6 Tinworth Street, London SE11 5AL, United Kingdom

Copyright © 2021 by The Rowman & Littlefield Publishing Group, Inc.

All rights reserved. No part of this book may be reproduced in any form or by any electronic or mechanical means, including information storage and retrieval systems, without written permission from the publisher, except by a reviewer who may quote passages in a review.

British Library Cataloguing in Publication Information Available

Library of Congress Cataloging-in-Publication Data

Names: Pickett Miller, Niya, 1982- editor.
Title: Sustaining black music and culture during COVID-19 : #Verzuz and Club Quarantine / edited by Niya Pickett Miller.
Description: Lanham : Lexington Books, 2021. | Includes bibliographical references and index. | Summary: "This book explores how pivotal Instagram Live events Club Quarantine and Verzuz have provided respite from social isolation and a rearticulated space for Black cultural engagement in the midst of the COVID-19 pandemic and increased racial tensions in the United States"Provided by publisher.
Identifiers: LCCN 2021028381 (print) | LCCN 2021028382 (ebook) | ISBN 9781793645043 (cloth) | ISBN 9781793645067 (paperback) | ISBN 9781793645050 (epub)
Subjects: LCSH: African AmericansMusicSocial aspects. | BlacksUnited StatesMusicSocial aspects. | Popular musicSocial aspectsUnited States. | Instagram (Electronic resource)Social aspects. | COVID-19 Pandemic, 2020Social aspects.
Classification: LCC ML3917.U6 S88 2021 (print) | LCC ML3917.U6 (ebook) | DDC 306.4/84240973dc23
LC record available at https://lccn.loc.gov/2021028381
LC ebook record available at https://lccn.loc.gov/2021028382

Mom, I can still hear Saturdays—you (frying fish while) playing R & B and the Blues—and Sundays—Gospel music (blasting) as you fixed my hair for church. Your music is the soundtrack for my fondest memories at home with you. Love always.

Contents

Foreword: "One Nation under a (Socially Distant) Groove"   ix
Eletra S. Gilchrist-Petty

1   Introduction   1
    Niya Pickett Miller

2   "Sisters in the name of Love": The Rhetorical Construction of Sisterhood in the Verzuz Challenges between Gladys Knight vs. Patti LaBelle and Erykah Badu vs. Jill Scott   9
    Goyland Williams and Mtalika Banda

3   Don't Take it Personal: Perceptions of Envy, Competitiveness, and Authenticity in the *Brandy v. Monica Verzuz Battle*   25
    Aisha Damali Lockridge and Janée N. Burkhalter

4   The Way We Were: How Black Women Created Space with Verzuz   41
    Kirstin Cheers

5   DJ's Gig: Affective Hip-Hop Culture and Affordances of Participatory Platforms during a Global Pandemic   57
    June Mia

6   Old Hits Verzuz New Technology: How a Pandemic Ushered Legacy Artists into Monetizing the Clout Economy   79
    Jabari Evans

7   Black and Quarantined: Celebrating Black Identity during COVID-19 via Instagram   95
    Katrina Overby, Gheni Platenburg, and Niya Pickett Miller

8 The Culture Wins: Continuing Black Cultural Traditions through Verzuz *Karl Lyn*	113
Conclusion *Niya Pickett Miller*	131
Index	135
About the Contributors	139

Foreword

"One Nation under a (Socially Distant) Groove"

Music has always been integral to the Black experience. The tribal melodies that were foundational to African ancestry were not quelled during the Middle passage. Out of the horrid conditions of slavery, Blacks unflinchingly embraced music as a means to easing their daily drudgery, sending up praises, and transporting coded messages to other slaves. Songs that emboldened slaves to "Follow the Drinking Gourd" eventually led them to the Civil Rights era. Songs akin to "We Shall Overcome" were used to peacefully seek justice and equality, while "Say it Loud—I'm Black and I'm Proud" not only spoke of Black beauty and empowerment but also provided a radical declaration against racial segregation and disenfranchisement.

At the 1964 Berlin Jazz Festival, Dr. Martin Luther King Jr. said in his opening address that "Jazz speaks for life. The blues tell the story of life's difficulties—and, if you think for a moment, you realize that they take the hardest realities of life and put them into music, only to come out with some new hope or sense of triumph. This is triumphant music."

The "triumphant music" Dr. King spoke of that provided a beacon of hope during the turbulent 1960s has persisted through time as a staple in the Black community, whether through mountain high or valley low experiences. With fists raised high in the air, modern-day demonstrators march and chant "Black Lives Matter" and "No Justice, No Peace" in protest of police brutality. Countless weddings, family reunions, and backyard barbecues are perceived as incomplete without a makeshift DJ spinning a tune to crowded dance floor. Despite the occasion, songs, chants, and melodies have served as historical and contemporary bonding forces among Blacks—until a global pandemic put a hard pause on the myriad of events that customarily brought so many together in a spirit of brother and sisterhood.

The COVID-19 pandemic began to plague the United States during the first quarter of 2020, halting most large events where Blacks gathered to commune, sing, dance, and fellowship. Not since 1918 had the United States experienced such a deadly and contagious virus, yet advancements in technology ignited a sense of resiliency and reimagined human engagement in ways previously deemed inconceivable. When quarantine and shelter-in-place mandates suspended large in-person musical gatherings Instagram was transformed into a prime digital space that ensured the beat went on.

Instagram's *Club Quarantine* (hosted by DJ D-Nice) and the *Verzuz* challenges (hosted by Timbaland and Swizz Beatz) provided much more than musical entertainment. These lyrical battles and pass-the-mic events soothed the singe of Covid fatigue by providing a sense of fellowship and cultural engagement housed in a virtual party atmosphere. In the 2020 conference presentation "Last Night a DJ Saved my Quarantine Life," a panel of scholars from the National Communication Association's Black Caucus described Instagram's virtual dance parities as providing metaphorical salvation during the COVID-19 pandemic.

Out of a lucid recognition of music's communicative power to unite and provide escapism, even under the most challenging of circumstances, this volume was birthed. Dr. Niya Pickett Miller has crafted a timely, provocative, and innovative volume that dissects the *Club Quarantine* and *Verzuz* battles. The contributors use a mix of theoretical approaches to explore diverse topics that span how Instagram's *Club Quarantine* and *Verzuz* promoted relationship maintenance, sparked collective memory, narratively bridged generational differences, and bolstered music as the cornerstone of Black culture. Through candid, authentic, and scholarly discourse, the volume speaks to how technology has reimagined dance parties in a quarantine world. While the pandemic has shifted many of our social activities, this volume serves an invaluable resource for anyone interested in learning more about the power of digital leisure spaces to bridge geographical distances, reinforce cultural practices, and keep us moving as "One Nation under a (socially distant) Groove."

Eletra S. Gilchrist-Petty, PhD
The University of Alabama in Huntsville

Chapter 1

Introduction

Niya Pickett Miller

I have not yet found one American that has not felt the sociocultural woes of the Coronavirus 19 (COVID-19) pandemic. Our relational dialectical need for autonomy/connection was more than achieved during 2020. This is mostly because our interpersonal engagement and customary ways of physically occupying spaces became increasingly (regulated and) distanced for our own survival. Notwithstanding, the profound sense of loss we all experienced through our personal or secondary associations to those with COVID-19 related illness and/or death, it was a tough year for many. The early days and months were especially challenging because we were not certain about the severity and longevity of the virus. Per the *American Journal of Managed Care* (AJMC, 2021), the United States' transition into *lockdown* during the first quarter of 2020 is punctuated by the following key events:

- January 31—World Health Organization declares COVID-19 a Global Health Emergency
- February 2—Global Air Travel Is Restricted
- February 3—U.S. Declares Public Health Emergency
- February 25—Center for Disease Control signals COVID-19 as a pandemic.
- March 6–21—passengers on a California cruise ship tests positive for COVID-19
- March 11—WHO Declares COVID-19 a Pandemic
- March 13—President Trump declared COVID-19 a national emergency
- March 19—California (the first state) issues a statewide stay-at-home order. Under this provision, all residents had to stay at home except for essential work, or shopping for essential needs. Moreover, health care systems had to prioritize services to those who were the sickest. Quickly, other states began to follow suit.

Progressively, the realities of the pandemic began to settle in. Soon, we all realized that COVID-19 was a serious matter. It (and no one) was going nowhere soon. Everything from vacation travel, baby showers, wedding ceremonies, school graduations, and even funerals experienced cancellations or (at minimum) a shift from the traditional close engagement, appearance, and feel that we were accustomed to.

Of course, the aforementioned chronological synopsis does not fully explicate the exponential life-shift the pandemic ushered in. There is a lot of global and domestic data, new discoveries, and noteworthy social and political events that (could be inserted to) expound the abbreviated timeline of the pandemic's impact on American society. Although, some of those details are mentioned in the subsequent chapters of this book; this collective work primarily discusses the communicative behaviors of Americans during the pandemic. More specifically, each chapter underscores the resilience of Black American culture during the United States' lockdown. COVID cooking (cooking during the pandemic), crisis nesting, comfort decorating, and home do it yourself (DIY) projects are just a few examples of creative and mental survival activities that have surged since the pandemic's onset. Like so many others, I also searched for stimulating, self-care activities during the pandemic, and music provided a soundtrack through it all.

Music has been solace for Blacks during the most tumultuous times in the past (e.g., slavery, Jim Crow), and the year 2020 was no different. Although large live music gatherings (e.g., indoor concerts, outdoor festivals) were halted, newer forms of musical togetherness—Club Quarantine (CQ) and Verzuz—were birthed via Instagram's (IG) Live feature, drawing large numbers of Black Americans (and others) to the social media platform. Both CQ and Verzuz showcased how technology and social media could be used to share the effervescent and corralling nature of Black music. Moreover, these virtual events provided a unique opportunity to safely experience, see, and express Black culture while in the confinements of quarantine. Moreover, we were able to solidify our togetherness, although survival mandated that we be apart. Truly, voluntary and mandated quarantining was (and remains) tough. However, it was increasingly difficult for so many to remain physically distant while the exigency of Black lives summoned public rallies for justice. Black people were reeling, and their creative cultural expressions (as usual) began to rise. As Gilyard and Banks (2018) have stated, "Black engagements with technologies . . . show in yet another way that African-American rhetoric reflects the struggles of living an existence that consistently vacillates between American Dream and American Nightmare, with some elements of both being always present" (p. 73). This is why our attention to the use of technology and social media as a novel approach toward Black culture during the onset and height of the COVID-19 spread in the

United States is particularly noteworthy. Admittingly, we authors are fans of CQ and Verzuz. However, we were (and continue) enjoying and witnessing significant cultural moments (CQ and Verzuz) within a significant cultural moment (COVID-19 pandemic). Hence, the idea for this book.

> We must range beyond instrumentalist views of technologies, beyond the idea that what matters with technology is only the device, the social-networking site, or the code that lies just beneath any digital interface. Technologies are interconnected systems of tools, politics, policies, labor, design, marketing, and use. Our view must be intersectional in its approaches to exigence and production, to call and response. Our view must also be multimodal in attempting to account for print, oral, visual, and performative. (Gilyard & Banks, 2018)

As COVID-19 survivors, observers, and communication scholars, we reflect on this specific historic time of uncertainty—where Black culture persisted during the pandemic, and forged ahead amid the killings of unarmed Black people (e.g., Ahmad Aurbrey, Breonna Taylor, George Floyd)—with critical thought. As we see it, the pandemic challenged typical engagement in Black culture, and technology—byway of social media—helped to fill the void caused by physical distancing. "Technological systems are . . . sites of Black agency, techne, knowledge, and creativity" (Gilyard & Banks, 2018). But what exactly is CQ and Verzuz? And what are the communicative influences and implications of these Black music events on Black culture?

CLUB QUARANTINE (CQ)

The original CQ and Verzuz began at the start of stay-at-home orders in March 2020, which effectively left many feeling bored and isolated in the United States. Binge watching television and scrolling through IG (to see who was doing whatever on Live) reached new heights. Many turned away from local and national news coverage that seemed to be squarely focused on the apocalyptic plague sweeping the planet. Amid the dismal press conferences and pandemic news stories were clips of people from Spain and Italy singing in solidarity on their balconies as a salute to healthcare and front-line workers. State-side, we saw images of New Yorkers applauding front-line workers each evening for their sacrificial efforts. Those outside of New York "watched and wondered where our own resolve lay" (Houghton, 2020, para. 4). We soon found it in the living room of D-Nice's Los Angeles home.

His sense of loneliness and isolation prompted casual conversation and music playing via IG's Live stream. In an interview with GQ, D-Nice explained, "I'm used to just being in front of so many people and being isolated was a difficult thing. Even though it ended up being for all of the people, initially it was more self-serving. It was just me wanting to play music and share stories with people" (Houghton, 2020, para. 7). D-Nice's livestreamed casual conversation and music sets morphed into a virtual celebrity hot spot. During the early days, D-Nice made calls to his celebrity friends, inviting them to drop in and provide extra inspiration for the viewers byway posting comments and emojis. In turn, D-Nice would give them shout-outs and acknowledge them as being "in the building." This gesture, of course, is reminiscent of typical in-person celebrity attention garnered in physical clubs. Invited celebrities jump on, and so have many others without prior invitations from D-Nice. "I mean I know J-Lo but not like *that*. I've met Drake . . . but they're not my friends, you know? They actually discovered it all on their own and came in, which was great, to know that the room was actually making a little bit of noise and that people wanted to be there," D-Nice explained in his interview with GQ (Houghton, 2020, para. 13). It (CQ) quickly became a virtual place "to be," and affectionately and effectively known as Club Quarantine.

VERZUZ

One quarantined night in March 2020, music super producer Timbaland hopped on IG Live, danced, and previewed records that he'd been creating while secluded in his studio. Timbaland, a Black man, is responsible for the iconic sound of beloved R & B princess, Aaliyah, and many of the award-winning hits from Missy Elliott, Justin Timberlake, and others. In the moment, he called out to Swizz Beats, another Black male super producer, "Where you at?" (Kennedy, 2020). The invitation led to a five-hour narrative and music-playing exchange between the two on IG Live. Timbaland and Swiss took turns playing their biggest hits and swapping stories as fans watched—loving every moment of what was unknowingly the first Verzuz "battle."

Notwithstanding the name, Verzuz is not (really) a competition with a winner and loser. But there is an evaluative dueling spirit wherein fans "keep score" through unofficial ranking of rounds of music. In the simplest of terms, Verzuz is a mashup of comparable music artists and creators narrating and playing their best productions and recordings in front of a virtual audience on IG Live. Rhetorically, it is a celebration of Black musical history and achievement, that encourages identification between the fans and artists. Framing Verzuz as a celebration has helped convince more private acts like Kenneth "Babyface" Edmonds to sign on, and secure the participation of female artists, who have historically been pitted against one another by the public such as Brandy and Monica (Kennedy, 2020).

Each event is situated as an intimate encounter that viewers are granted participatory access to. The shared vignettes (about the origins and iterations of songs that were minimally known), and the viewers' live comment thread help to construct the familiar nature of each event. *Verzuz* made uneventful weekends and monotonous weeknights fun again under the guise of a spirited of friendly competition all while reminding and in some cases, teaching viewers about the nuances of a hit record and the real-life encounters shared between the featured artists.

Both CQ and Verzuz are highly successful music listening events that have cocreated experience culturally comparable to the "Black cookout" or "family reunion,"—allowing everyday folks to party with A-list celebrities from Hollywood, music, sports, and politics. Because both events have become significant spaces to reach captive Black audiences during the pandemic, it is important to understand the communicative potential of Club Quarantine and the Verzuz. Therefore, the following chapters offer analyses of these events using disparate methodologies and applied communication theories and frameworks.

THE CHAPTERS

Chapter 2, "'Sisters in the name of Love': The Rhetorical Construction of Sisterhood in the Verzuz Challenges between Gladys Knight vs. Patti Labelle and Erykah Badu vs. Jill Scott" (Goyland Williams & Mtalika Banda, University of Massachusetts Amherst), examines the performance of Black women's friendship exhibited during the Verzuz challenges. Williams and Banda lean on Black feminist studies, hip-hop studies, and studies of Black popular culture to uncover and describe how Black women construct meaningful relationships with each other, and build communal exchanges in environments intrinsically designed to generate and maintain hostility and rivalry between them. The authors argue that Black women's intransigent performances of camaraderie and pact-mentality circumvented the expectations of a virtual battle of sorts during the season one Verzuz challenges. Instead, Black women's communication and behavior during the Verzuz challenges offer a revised narrative about the cultural script for Black women and their (non)pugnacious nature.

In chapter 3, Aisha Damali Lockridge and Janée N. Burkhalter (Saint Joseph's University) attend to Verzuz the battle featuring 1990s Black teen sensations, Brandy Norwood and Monica Arnold (known by their monikers Brandy and Monica). Their chapter, "Don't Take It Personal: Perceptions of Envy, Competitiveness, and Authenticity in the *Brandy v. Monica Verzuz* Battle," situates the former teen-queen battle as an act of inheritance that motivated scrutiny of the socially constructed bitterness and rivalry between (and around) the women. Through their analysis, a more nuanced understanding of how publicly manufactured and legitimate competitiveness influenced the past and current perception of Brandy and Monica's—young Black female— relationship(s).

To round off the gendered critiques of the Verzuz battles is chapter 4, "The Way We Were: How Black Women Created Space with Verzuz" (Kirstin Cheers, University of Memphis). In it, Cheers analyzes the battles' intergenerational viewership among Black women and identifies "Black woman rhetoric" as a particular vernacular used by Black women to define their womanhood and navigate the COVID-19. Cheers argues that Black women, with their colloquial speech, are embraced by audiences of various demographics especially during political and social uncertainty. Moreover, through the female Verzuz challenges, Black women created enclaves for Black women viewers to congregate and disconnect from the white and patriarchal hegemony they currently survive within.

The remaining chapters explore how livestreamed Black music events have influenced socioeconomics and digital leisure during the pandemic. In chapter 5, "DJ's Gig: Affective Hip-Hop Culture and Affordances of Participatory Platforms during a Global Pandemic" (June Mia, University of Illinois), the author utilizes quantitative and qualitative methods to analyze DJs' use of participatory platforms to understand how their work changed during the COVID-19 pandemic. Several theories (i.e., gig economy, affordances, relational labor, and participatory platforms) are explicated and applied to the experience of D-Nice's #ClubQuarantine. June Mia describes how DJs like CQ's D-Nice, have reimagined affordances, or gigs by becoming more active on social media platforms during a time when traditional music-themed spaces (e.g., clubs, festivals) were limited. D-Nice's (and others) ability to pivot the work of DJ-ing toward social media livestreaming has resulted in supplementary and even primary income sources for this specific artistic work.

Chapter 6, "Old Hits Verzuz New Technology: How a Pandemic Ushered Legacy Artists into Monetizing the Clout Economy" (Jabari Evans, Northwestern University), explores patterns of music streaming and social media usage during the early Verzuz battles. Additionally, the chapter theorizes about how the livestreamed music performances can drive a new model of music monetization. Evans locates Verzuz as an example of how virtual concerts can trigger artist exposure, revenue, and record listening in a moment when audience members cannot attend in-person music concerts—but are far more engaged with social media for collective listening. Katrina Overby (Rochester Institute of Technology), Gheni Platenburg (Auburn University), and Niya Pickett Miller (Samford University) recognize the significance and process of Black connectivity through CQ and Verzuz in chapter 7, aptly titled "Black and Quarantined: Celebrating Black Identity During COVID-19 via Instagram." In their discussion, IG is positioned as a multigenerational digital leisure space that rhetorically sustains American Black culture, identity, and community during the COVID-19 pandemic. The authors view IG's livestreaming function as a chronicling of the Black lived experience during a challenging social climate of particular political, racial, physical, and mental anguish.

In chapter 8, "The Culture Wins: Continuing Black Cultural Traditions through Verzuz" (Karl Lyn University of Massachusetts Amherst), critical methodology combined with textual analysis—TRIOS model—is used to examine the Verzuz battles. Lyn argues that Verzuz renders Black people an opportunity to operate from a position of sociocultural power by saturating the IG Live events with Afrocentric values about time, rhythm, improvisation, orality, and spirituality (TRIOS). Each of these elements help to construct Verzuz as a cultural resource wherein Black people orient themselves toward communal legacies while mitigating multiple adversities. This chapter contributes to the growing body of literature on Black popular culture and technological literacies by showing how Black people utilize digital media to disseminate and access culturally affirming experiences.

Concertedly, these chapters expound the myriad of possibilities for understanding the communicative and cultural significance of CQ and the Verzuz battles during the Coronavirus pandemic in the United States. We want this collective to spark further scholarship that expands our start here. While these livestreamed music events have distracted and entertained us, we have elucidated how CQ and Verzuz are not just "another thing or things to look at." But rather, these events are buttressing, propelling, *and* reframing Black popular culture. The varying frameworks and approaches demonstrated in this book demonstrate how communication theory can be applied to contemporary Black phenomena. Read this collection from cover to cover or by random chapter selection. Regardless of your reading preference, I hope that you enjoy this curated collection and discover how Black culture wins, despite so much loss in 2020. During and/or after your reading, consider grabbing your smart device, dusting off your dancing shoes, and joining the next Live event. As D-Nice often says in CQ, *It's a vibe!*

REFERENCES

AJMC Staff. (2021). A Timeline of COVID-19 Developments in 2020. Retrieved from https://www.ajmc.com/view/a-timeline-of-covid19-developments-in-2020

Gilyard, K., & Banks, A. J. (2018). On African-American Rhetoric. Routledge. Ebook. Retrieved from https://bookshelf.vitalsource.com/books/9781351610636

Houghton, E. (2020). How D-Nice United a Socially Isolated World With Club Quarantine. *GQ* Online. Retrieved from https://www.gq.com/story/d-nice-interview-2020

Kennedy, G. D. (2020). Inside the Unstoppable Rise of Verzuz. *GQ* Online. Retrieved from https://www.gq.com/story/verzuz-oral-history

Chapter 2

"Sisters in the name of Love"

The Rhetorical Construction of Sisterhood in the Verzuz Challenges between Gladys Knight vs. Patti LaBelle and Erykah Badu vs. Jill Scott

Goyland Williams and Mtalika Banda

Nearly thirty-five years after their now classic 1986 concert, "Sisters in the Name of Love," Gladys Knight and Patti LaBelle captured the attention of more than half a million (concurrent) viewers and a reported 1.2 million total viewers—who tuned in from Apple TV and Apple Music—to watch what Mikki Kendall (2020) has referred to as "one of the greatest, possibly defining, cultural events of the pandemic era . . ." (para. 1). Additionally, LaBelle and Knight's performance was the second highest tweeted battle, following behind Brandy and Monica (Gunn, 2020). As one of the many competitions organized by Swizz Beatz and Timbaland under the Verzuz umbrella, the Patti LaBelle and Gladys Knight showcase did not disappoint.

As viewers across the world tuned in from their digital platforms to listen to and for LaBelle's "spellbinding screams" and Knight's bluesy ballads, the Godmother and Empress of Soul (as they have been rightfully dubbed) sat perched on the stage of the Fillmore Philadelphia where they sang each other's greatest hits, bragged about their culinary exploits, and recalled fond memories of their personal and professional lives. True to its name, "One Night Only" felt like a final public tribute to two legendary singers who have sang and danced their way into our hearts and homes for more than forty years. Rather than a competition between two legendary figures in American and Black music circles, they collectively demonstrated the transformative power of Black women's friendship and culture affirming sensibilities that are inevitably tethered to Black expressive culture.

In the same ways that LaBelle and Knight were able to bring a generation of Black women together, Erykah Badu and Jill Scott were able to achieve a similar space for a younger generation of Black women and Black folks who listened to and/or grew up on Hip-Hop and R&B. As the first versus challenge that only featured women, Badu's and Scott's performance was watched in real time by more than seven hundred thousand people. At the time, their Verzuz was the most streamed virtual event that producers Swizz Beatz and Timbaland had held up until that point. Indeed, what these two women showcased in their performance were not simply battles, but genuine expressions of Black womanhood and sisterhood to be exact. As the title of a *Texas Monthly* article proclaims, "Erykah Badu and Jill Scott's Verzuz Battle Felt More Intimate Than a Live Show" (Oyeniyi, 2020). Many of the folks watching grew up to these women, and it is very plausible Erykah and Jill were aware of this when they agreed to do this Verzuz challenge. While most of the battles that occurred prior to theirs carried a competitiveness and energy that—although conducive to much of the Hip-Hop community—placed more emphasis on competition than community, with Badu and Scott, many of us saw and felt a shift in what a virtual battle could represent even through digital mediums. Informed by their "distinct confidence and spirituality," it is clear that Jill and Erykah adored and celebrated each other's blackness and womanhood (Oyeniyi, 2020, para. 4). Thus, it was not surprising that their decades-long communal centered and Black woman affirming performances had primed their followers that this would be nothing less than a Erykah Badu and Jill Scott collaboration.

Given the overwhelmingly positive appraisals and testimonies of the Badu vs. Scott and Knight vs. LaBelle challenges as clear outliers from the other Verzuz battles (both male and female), it is notable that their "collaborative praxis" (Kernodle, 2014, p. 30) and not their efforts to adhere to the standards of competition set them apart as artists. More urgently, it was their ability to transcend the trappings of what Hip-Hop heads refer to as "beef"—or what the linguist Geneva Smitherman (2006) more pointedly characterizes as "conflict, squabble, a problem" that facilitated a model of Black music and popular culture excellence that is rooted in community, collaboration, and celebration (p. 22). Put simply, these four women repeatedly emphasized their friendship and solidarity with one another over and against what the ethnomusicologist, Tammy Kernodle (2014) characterizes as the "male competitive spirit" (p. 28). Consequently, they turned "the game" on its proverbial head by their conscious decision to contest popular culture's obsession with tropes of hostility, competitiveness, and even violence (verbal or otherwise).

In this chapter, we argue that these four women's display of care and charisma rhetorically functioned as a counternarrative to negative tropes and stereotypes that too often characterize Black women's relationship to each other. Those tropes include but are not limited to the Sapphire figure or the pernicious Black woman who is often thought to be loud, angry, and perpetually in conflicts or drama with their peers and counterparts (Yarborough & Bennett, 2000). Whereas other battles featured actual beef—such as Brandy vs. Monica and Gucci Mane vs. Jeezy, these four women brought positive vibes and a deep sense of love for their community and each other at a vulnerable time for the nation and more acutely for Black America. What is more significant is that Jill Scott and Erykah Badu and Patti La Belle and Gladys Knight openly affirmed their commitment to each other's careers and livelihoods over and against the logics that sought to pit them against each other for most of their careers is notable in particular.

Instead of succumbing to these thin constructions of competition and scarcity—the narrative that there can only be one great artist at a time—these four women were interrupting and disrupting paradigms of polarization and competitiveness that has shaped and textured Black music in general and R&B in particular. In particular, we argue that the successful and highly celebrated displays of community—and more specifically Black sisterhood was created—not by the terms and conditions of the Verzuz challenge, but in spite of them. This collaborative spirit was a central point of discussion on social media sites, in households, across popular culture circles, and within publications is in itself an important discussion.

Beyond demonstrating the power and potency of Black women's friendship and music, this chapter probes the depths of Black entertainment and (counter) publics as a vehicle for examining what Kalamu ya Salaam (1995) articulates as the oppositional nature of Black music and culture. As he writes, Great Black Music (GBM) is both a "break with the status quo yet an extension of tradition . . ." (p. 355). We argue then, that the "break" that is employed in these two Verzuz challenges functioned as a way to build and reimagine community in times of conflict, both personal and social. Building on scholarship in Black feminist studies, Hip-Hop studies, and Black popular culture, this chapter reflects upon the performative dynamic of Black women's friendship in the context of the Verzuz challenges. In particular, we analyze Patti LaBelle vs. Gladys Knight and the Erykah Badu vs. Jill Scott Verzuz in order to examine the ways that Black women construct meaningful relationships with other women, and thereby, participate in building community in spaces designed to foster antagonistic competition. Finally, we argue that as Black popular culture icons who have increasingly navigated social and professional circles predicated on fierce competition, that these women's subversive performances of solidarity and friendship supplanted the expectations of a musical virtual battle. In exploring the rhetorical and performative constructions that these singers/artists employed in the Verzuz challenge, we ask: How does Black women's artistic practice (in this instance: the Verzuz challenge) operate as both a homeplace (after bell hooks) for Black women and simultaneously disrupts traditional constructions of competition and gendered performances of masculinity?

SITUATING CLUB QUARANTINE AND THE VERZUZ CHALLENGE

Inspired by the Hip-Hop icons and premiere music producers, Swizz Beatz and Timbaland, the Verzuz concept connotes the battles that took place between emcees, b-boys and b-girls. It also connotes predominantly male-dominated spaces that Hip-Hop was brought up in. For the most part, this competitive masculine energy has dominated most of the Verzuz challenges during quarantine leading up to "Erykah Badu vs. Jill Scott." From the narratives on Twitter and Instagram, virtually all the Verzuz have been performed with the idea that a winner will be decided, much to Swizz and Timbaland's plan.

The format is set up with rounds in which each artist shares a song, and the fans decide who won each round. In the "battle" between Babyface and Teddy Riley, this competitive model made for light-hearted banter and commentary in which fans made fun of Riley's technical difficulties. On the other hand, but also we see how close to danger the Verzuz challenges could be when we look at the potential beef that was permeated between rappers T.I. and 50 Cent over just the idea of a challenge. In that battle, both rappers went too far on social media in how they were making fun of one another, especially considering the bloody history and tension that these two rappers share between each other. Given that Hip-Hop culture was in part birthed and shaped by raw and sometimes unbridled competitiveness—that sometimes manifested at each competitor taking sly jabs at the other—anyone who knows this should understand how quickly manufactured beef can turn into real beef. Thus, when Erykah and Jill chose to promote their event by playing each other's music on social media, they were starting a new tradition to Verzuz in which they asked fans not to pit them against each other, but to celebrate both women for their shared brilliance.

"VERZUZ" AND THE BLACK DIGITAL PUBLIC SPHERE

When the sudden outbreak of Covid-19 and the subsequent surge of deaths across the country demanded that we go into isolation, many of our notions of being and participating in community were abruptly upended. No longer able to safely socialize or attend concerts, sporting events, clubs, family gatherings, or just everyday activities, one could logically reason that more people were turning toward increased social media usage and digital platforms as a way to feel some semblance of connection. In times of conflict and crisis, as Pryor and Outley (2020) have noted: "Digital space is a place for healing and transformation, where a communal language is created" (p. 4).

Consistent with what some scholars have characterized as the digital nature of the contemporary Black public sphere (Everett, 2002; Brock, 2012; Duthely, 2017), where Black people sustain community through cultural discourses, we insist that social media sites such as Instagram, Twitter, Apple TV, and YouTube offer a glimpse into the ways that alternative spaces reimagine ways of being and doing. In its commitments to "not be shut out of or pushed away from the public sphere" (Pough, 2004, p. 17), these Black counterpublics operate and function as a way to elevate and highlight what Roderick Graham and Shawn Smith (2016) describe in their essay "The Content of Our #Characters: Black Twitter as Counterpublic" as "iconic sites for the production of uniquely black discourses" (p. 435).

However, despite the liberatory and transformational possibilities of Black (counter)publics, they are not immune from issues that impact vulnerable members of any public sphere. For even in these culturally Black spaces that are seemingly affirming and inclusive of marginalized voices within their ranks, issues which acutely impact women of color are frequently relegated to their own silos or subsumed under categories which always already imagine the public sphere as a male-dominated space. The "Verzuz" challenges afforded Black music fans the opportunity to connect with others through a shared space of heightened vulnerability. Influenced in part by what some scholars refer to as the Black public sphere, Black artists—especially women in this instance—craft spaces where they can reimagine ways of being and doing in the face of considerable odds. Said another way, people can engage in subversive acts to reimagine ways of being in the face of marginalization and other forms of oppressions. As Gwendolyn Pough (2004) asserts: Black women have often been at the forefront of building radical counterstories and ideologies that are more capacious and she writes:

> In ways that we have yet to fully recognize and acknowledge, Black women have helped to shape and build the Black public sphere as we know it. They have shaped the public sphere so much that I would add the caveat that we can no longer simply say that the women were present. We need to articulate fuller accounts of their voices and their work . . . We need to extend our interrogations and discussions in ways that validate not only the presence of women in the Black public sphere but women's roles in shaping that sphere. (p. 37)

Read through this frame, both Badu and Scott in addition to Patti LaBelle and Gladys Knight showcase the sheer beauty and resistance to dominant scripts that Black women take up when they choose friendship and intimacy in spaces where they are "supposed" to viciously compete against each other for all the culture to see and bear witness to. Instead, these women brought their musical genius, impeccable fashion styles, and opened up space for millions of followers to rejoice in times of suffering through their art and visibility as culture bearers. Further, their gendered performances of intimacy not only showcased the fact that collaboration is not only possible across digital mediums and generational divides but also that Black women can bring the proverbial heat without trying to diminish each other in the process.

BLACK SISTERHOOD AS SOLIDARITY AND PERFORMATIVE HEALING

Even in the company of other women, Black women are pushed out of collective imaginings of womanhood and consequently, sisterhood and care. Steeped in sexism, classism, and racism, healthy notions of Black sisterhood and female friendships are threatened by values that pit these women against each other. Rather than operating from a space of collective resistance to structural oppression and marginalization, Black women are encouraged to mimic male supremacist thinking and thereby consent to rhetorics of scarcity and lack that uphold antagonisms and rivalries.

In her 1986 article "Sisterhood: Political solidarity between women," bell hooks insists that bonding among women is often a difficult political project because of sexism, racism, classism, "and a host of other prejudices" (hooks, p. 128). For hooks, women are susceptible to internalizing sexist thinking and politics which leads to frameworks and postures of male supremacist thinking. She writes: "Between women, male supremacist values are expressed through suspicious, defensive, competitive behaviour. It is sexism that leads women to feel threatened by one another without cause" (hooks, p. 129). As a result, social and political appeals to sisterhood among women often fall flat when they do not account for the ways that women experience common oppressions and the ways in which they are distinct. In calling out the ways in which "bourgeois white women" mobilize supremacist thinking against other out-group women, bell hooks suggests that bonding through a presumably shared notion of sisterhood is not a given fact for Black women (hooks, p. 127).

Whereas hooks (1986) contends that womanhood and sisterhood are insufficient categories for political organizing given the sharp ideological differences across race, class, and gendered ways of knowing, Marnel Goins (2011) amplifies the ways that Black women use friendship as a way to navigate their own lives and the larger society. She writes:

> Group friendships are one space where Black women have the freedom to express and construct themselves and to negotiate group segregation and integration. Through the telling of stories in these groups, women conceptualize their friendship as a unique homeplace in which to freely voice their opinion and be themselves. (p. 545)

Goins assessment of Black women's friendship as a homeplace is insightful for considering how Black women artists negotiate the demands of the music industry and their personal lives. Given that Hip-Hop and Black music circles in general has frequently been assessed as a space where rivalries—whether real or imagined—run rampant, competition is the name of the game. Although typically reserved for male rappers who sometimes position themselves in direct opposition to particular individuals and or groups, Black women artists are not immune from this framework of competitive antagonism. The examples abound. As such, the Verzuz challenge between these four women highlights the ways that defiance and resistance can be mobilized to create and reimagine what Black music and digital spaces can be.

As seen on Twitter and Instagram in particular, viewers collectively saw the ways that collaboration and friendship are powerful tools in fostering spaces for healing and remembering the best of the Black tradition. As Marnel Goins (2011) contends: "These friendship groups allow the females to speak with freedom, to strengthen their souls, and to tell stories that reinforce their identities, particularly in a society that magnifies their differences" (p. 532). Similar to Knight and LaBelle's articulation of their decades-long friendship, we insist that Badu and Scott have simply continued in this tradition. From our assessment, while the appeals to a Black communal ethos were an essential staple undergirding the entirety of the Verzuz challenges, it was the performances of Jill Scott vs. Erykah Badu and Patti LaBelle vs. Gladys Knight that served as the templates of what healthy competition can and should be.

SISTERS IN THE NAME OF LOVE: OR, WHEN BLACK WOMEN SING

Minutes into their 1986 performance at the historic Aquarius Theater in Los Angeles—appropriately titled *Sisters In The Name of Love*—Dionne Warwick openly lamented the fact that it had taken so long for her, Patti LaBelle, and Gladys Knight to perform together. As she declared:

We have known each other a long, long time . . . We've always talked about doing this. We've wanted to get together. We never had the opportunity. We've done it on buses as we traveled on tours. We've done it in our cars. But we never been on the same stage to do it. (*Sisters in the Name of Love*, 1986)

Drawing on their close relationship as friends and colleagues, Dionne Warwick provided a narrative that constructed an ethos of familiarity. A familiarity that not only spoke to the unique challenges that come with maintaining a high-profile professional music career, but also doing this while trying to cultivate meaningful bonds. Consequently, these three legendary singers collectively underscored the power of Black women's commitment to each other, and to coming together despite various social and personal exigencies. They demonstrate that Black women's friendship and art serve as a powerful mechanism for highlighting the richness of Black creative expression.

Across six decades, their collective—but very personal—sojourns through Black music circles; their shared history as Black women of a particular social, cultural, and political moment highlights the ways that publics influence artists and vice versa. Embodying the aesthetics and comportment of Black women who have been designated with the honorific of "auntie"—Auntie Gladys, Auntie Patti, Auntie Dionne—or those Black women who Mark Anthony Neal (2020) describe as "women who continue to hold an important place in the culture"—LaBelle, Knight, and Warwick positioned themselves as an unbreakable sisterhood (para. 6). As evidenced by their gestures, body language, and (sonic) intimacy with one another, these three women did more than vocalize their bond, but lived out what it means for a group of Black women to create intentional spaces of personal and professional fulfillment. "The result," as Maureen Mahon (2020) declared, "was the creation of a black women's space that visualized and sounded out 'the power of the erotic' . . . a space that was occupied and controlled by women who did not seem to require the presence of men for fulfillment" (p. 198). Although their performance in 1986 was "inventively staged" as get TV reports, few would question the authenticity of their collective bond and genuine feelings toward each other. Theirs was a friendship that had and would withstand the test of times. Thus, when Gladys Knight, Patti LaBelle, and Dionne Warwick graced the stage of the Aquarius theatre more than thirty-five years ago—where they crooned and belted out some of their greatest hits—one thing was certain: they had collectively joined the line of foremothers who saw their survival and careers as intertwined.

Discussing personal issues that range from single parenthood, relationship woes, and body image, what becomes clear and visible up front is that their friendship was "more than a casual relationship" (*Sisters in the name of love*, 1986). It was clear that the trio had weathered many proverbial storms together. Indeed, they were "sista friends" (Seymour, 2020). That these women had forged an abiding love and mutual affection for each other as well as their respective families is nothing to scoff at; especially considering the ways that public culture—the music industry in particular—often profits from discord and division among celebrities.

Upon the occasion of the 2020 Verzuz challenge, Gladys Knight and Patti LaBelle took the stage of the Fillmore in Philadelphia in a reunion of sorts for the Verzuz challenge. It was where they would share music from their respective catalogues, recall a time long passed, while audiences could witness their musical gifts through Instagram, YouTube, and the Verzuz website. As one of the many events under the Verzuz umbrella, Patti LaBelle vs. Gladys Knight did not disappoint. As the world stood in pause due to the rapid spread of the COVID-19 virus, for many, these Verzuz challenges served an essential function: they gave Black folks hope and connection, even if they could not leave their homes.

For Knight and LaBelle, the vibe that began the night felt like a cookout or family reunion. It was as if the DJ was urging viewers to get up in their living rooms and do the electric slide before these two sisters came out on screen. For almost ten minutes music played as fans logged into the Instagram Live event. Black celebrities–the likes of Octavia Spencer, Kerry Washington, Quest Love, Brandy, Lena Waithe, Jennifer Hudson, Oprah Winfrey, and Michelle Obama, to name a few—commented on their excitement of being able to both witness what was sure to be a legendary show of the greats and collectively celebrate with more than a half a million fans on Instagram Live. As many rightfully noted: this was both a history lesson and a necessary balm. When LaBelle and Knight finally did come on stage, they simply sat down and immediately began speaking to one another as if they were continuing a conversation that had been decades in the making. Perhaps they were.

After a few minutes of talking and "catching up," Patti LaBelle can be heard telling the production team to turn the fan away from her hair. However, unbeknownst to both Patti and Gladys, the Live recording had already begun. Meanwhile, on the Versus TV channel of Instagram Live, fans quickly took note of their fashion choices, lively conversation, and the legendary nature of what was to come. The Oprah Magazine Instagram account—@oprahmagazine—wrote: "The sequins! The mirrors! Hasn't even started and we're living for this already" (2020, September 14)! When they were finally mic'd up, they quickly began to talk about how close they were and how their friendship had endured through good times and bad times. LaBelle turns to Gladys Knight and says, "We've been together for years and years and years! . . . I know we did a lot together . . . And had fun doing it . . . OG Style!" Noting the ways that they had been separated for so long since their traveling days.

LaBelle noted: "There's about 150 years up here that we're sharing . . . This is like a blessing for me to be here with you . . . after so many years apart."

Gladys Knight—in a move that seemed to not only validate what Patti LaBelle was saying, but to insert her own contribution—explained to viewers that "we actually grew up together." Knight even remembered when LaBelle first began to sing and form her own band. While they were reminiscing about the past—of being pregnant at the same time, raising kids, and now cherishing their roles as grandmothers and great-grandmothers—fans could sense the maternal presence and deep camaraderie that had been established throughout the years. At one point both Patti LaBelle and Gladys Knight talked about their "cooking fever" (Gladys Knight) and famous culinary skills and how they prepared big meals even though they no longer had children living at home. Banana pudding, mac and cheese, collard greens, cornbread, and of course, Patti's famous sweet potato pies were a topic of discussion both in their conversation and on social media. What was evident and well documented on social media platforms is that LaBelle and Knight had set the tone for a night of intergenerational knowledge-sharing and living. The comments prove such a point.

"JILLY FROM PHILLY" VS. ERYKAH BADU

When Swizz Beatz wrote on the #Verzuz Instagram page, "It's time for the Queens to represent. [Erykah Badu] vs. [Jill Scott] the paperwork is in [Timbaland]" (Verzuz, 2020), Black folk knew a tone of sisterhood would come through. This is how Black audiences first received a Verzuz between Badu and Scott, with the chance to witness two Black queens engaging in a royal conversation. For those who grew up in the barbershops, hair salons, on the block, or in Black public spaces, these two icons are central staples to Black cultural production in general and Black music in particular.

Make no mistake, Badu and Scott coming together was not a competition, but a deep bond and collaboration that had been forged and strengthened through years and fans took note. On *Essence*, Joi-Marie Mckenzie acknowledges how fans positioned themselves to receive this event, with DJ First Class writing on Twitter "There can be no winner. I refuse" (DJ First Class, 2020). Christian Allaire writes, "But Scott and Badu's battle—which lasted almost twenty rounds of songs—was entirely different, in that it was less of a traditional 'battle' and more of a collaboration—it simply felt like two friends trading songs and vibing off of each other, versus competing" (Allaire, 2020, para. 2). Allaire highlights the responses on Twitter and other social media: "That wasn't Jill VS Erykah, that was Jill & Erykah," wrote one Twitter user of the uplifting stream. "They tore down the *battle* model and held space for love, affirmation, and sisterhood," wrote another user. "We could all learn from tonight" Director Ava Duverney wrote on Twitter, "The joy of blackness was deeply felt today, and I needed that light, that love, that community the way only we do it. Blessings and beauty to the Queens Erykah Badu and Jill Scott. The harmony hope and humanity you shared tonight was simply exquisite" (Allaire, 2020, para. 3).

Sisterhood defined their night, and it ain't hard to tell. One can look to how they both chose to open up the Verzuz, recounting the song that had first introduced them to one another: "You Got Me." A record by the live Hip-Hop band The Roots, which Erykah sings the hook on, but what they both reminisce on is how it was actually written by a young Jill Scott. Erykah remembers when she first heard the song, and recalls being blown away upon hearing an unknown and young Jill Scott's voice. Erykah claims that right after listening, she turns to Quest Love, leader of The Roots, and says, "Well what imma do with it?" implying how complete Ms. Scott's interpretation of the song was. Jill then shares with Erykah (and viewers) that it was the first song she had ever written:

> I'm sure you know, but you gave me—The Roots gave me—my first opportunity . . . to write anything ever. It's the first song I ever wrote. Ever. And it's the hook. But I had never written anything. Quest was like 'what's up? Can you do this?' And I lied . . . and for you—Queen Badu—to sing words that I wrote, and I don't think you ever done that again. Everything else you've written yourself. I'm so honored.

Jill was just happy someone like Erykah, a well-known name by that point, would even consider singing on a track written by some unknown songwriter the world would soon know as "Jilly from Philly." It would be understandable to assume that perhaps Erykah Badu chose "You Got Me" to set a tone for what would follow as a beautiful night of two Black women celebrating one another in sisterhood. After all, Erykah has an extensive music catalog under her name alone and she could have chosen any track she had written herself. Instead, Erykah choses a song she only sings the hook on, and which someone else wrote. For those who have followed either of these women's careers may have wondered how both Erykah and Jill felt about this arrangement— a song which Jill initially wrote, but that Erykah popularized and became known for singing. Perhaps Erykah starts with this song to invite us into their shared space. "You Got Me" represents Jill Scott's entry into the music industry but also one that solidified Erykah's relationship to The Roots, her place within the Soulquarian movement, Hip-Hop, and the culture. This song is not only simply a point of departure into their relationship but also a statement to viewers that says this is not a battle, but a performance in mutual admiration.

Later in the Verzuz, Erykah is speaking to Jill, but we know that she is also including the audience, when she asks Jill to remember their history as friends stating: "I don't think people know how much we talk on the phone and work out our things and talk through these relationships and these children and childbirth and all this kind of stuff. Are you over there crying again?" There is a smirk on Erykah's face, telling viewers this is not the first time these two women have moved one another to tears. Viewers learn that from the very beginning they both had respect for one another, but like Patti LaBelle and Gladys Knight, Jill reminds Erykah how the media continually attempted to pit them against one another. "They pitted us against each other for a long time. A very long time. From the beginning, it's been some kind of stink in the air. That didn't belong to neither of us. I'm glad to squash that for all of you."

By the end of this Verzuz, we know that they never chose a narrative that said two women pioneers should be in opposition to one another. Nor a narrative that said two Black women in a male-dominated industry could not be friends. They tell viewers that from their first encounters, they each were determined to build their sister up. This Verzuz is a chance to witness the depths of their decades-long sisterhood. The depths of their bond and commitment to each other are made explicitly clear. We see it in the intro, when they are sharing stories of mothering during a global pandemic. Jill shares what helping her son in remote learning has taught her. "I'm learning to be patient with him," she says to Erykah, "and he's learning to be patient with me."

They do not simply honor each other; they bring in all the Black women and men who paved the way for their own creativity. At one point Erykah asks Jill what inspired her to start writing, and Jill remembers back to a high school English teacher:

> She asked us to write an essay about anyone we wanted. Just close your eyes and point. She had a list, and I landed on Nikki Giovanni. And it opened my mind and blew my wig back, cause I had never seen myself on paper before. And after that, the door just opened: Langston Hughes, James Baldwin, just beautiful—Sonia Sanchez! All these amazing writers that could paint me with words, that's how it started.

The tradition Scott and Badu hail from was built on the foundation of so many Black creatives, and to see Jill place her own creative birth in relation to these giants shows an awareness of their own race, gender, and how to best create a space that makes that known to the audience. For the real fans, these are the moments they pray for—where two creative geniuses in their own right are sitting still to ask each other questions and to listen to each other share a little bit of themselves. Badu and Scott are doing this with not just one another, but over half a million viewers.

How was this event able to transcend the previous Verzuz in the fact that fans had no interest in pitting these icons against one another? Maybe it was the fact that when promoting this event on their individual Instagram accounts, Jill and Erykah decided to both post videos of themselves singing the other's music, highlighting their respect for each other's craft. Maybe it was the gospel that played for fifteen minutes, sprinkled with poems by Nikki Giovanni, as the audience waited for the Queens to enter the room. Or maybe, as Celeste Doaks writes, "what truly set this 'battle' apart were the words of wisdom and the confessions shared between the songs. These women, mothers and mutual friends were ultimately way more interested in connecting than battling" (Doaks, 2020, para. 11). In two and a half hours, they shared themselves with Black folk, and they listened. Black folk listened as these two women shared stories of family, mothering, and their own friendship over the years.

What remained clear both during and after Badu and Scott's Verzuz challenge was that this was not their first rodeo in how to navigate male-dominated spaces as Black women with grace, for their careers were defined by it. A story that could have been shared was the media uproar that surrounded the 2001 *Soul Train* awards, where Erykah Badu was the projected winner for Best R&B/Soul Album of the Year by a solo artist, but with which Jill Scott took the award home for her album *Who is Jill Scott?* The confusion was that journalists' press releases had Badu as the winner, so did the printed winners' sheets at the event. Along with them announcing Badu was the winner in the live tapping. It was later that "a crestfallen statement came from the event organizers that a mistake had been made and Jill Scott's *Who Is Jill Scott?* was in fact the winner" (McIver, 2002, p. 233). Even though the media ran with the story and attempted to pit them against each in the wake of this error, Badu and Scott remained unphased from the matter, and never felt a need to address it. If they would not compete against each other in 2001, then it should be no surprise they chose to make this Verzuz space one of celebration.

As Jill Scott reminisce on their decade's long friendship, their #Verzuz was a successful attempt at "the creation of a digital counterpublic [that] allows for the assertion Black humanity and resistance from multiple and varied voices" (Duthely, 2017, p. 204). Jill Scott and Erykah Badu were doing the work of making these Verzuz something that perhaps Timbaland and Swizz Beatz did not intend. Their sisterhood wrecked the norm of the competitive drive these Verzuz were becoming known for.

BY WAY OF CONCLUSION

Years from now, we might be telling one of those "where were you when . . ." stories about that time that Swizz Beatz and Timbaland brought back some of the greatest contemporary Black artists to grace the American music landscape. And in my (re)telling, I would hope to say that I was a witness to Gladys Knight and Patti LaBelle coming together for a highly publicized Verzuz battle. And when (re) telling that story I might land on a number of memorable moments that "sent me up"—to borrow a Black vernacular phrase—moments that further solidified their rightful places in Black popular music history. Whether it was the Apple sponsored advertisements featuring these two divas' whipping up some of their favorite recipes in the kitchen; reminiscing over the times of old, or how their music sent us to a simpler time. The same can be said for Erykah Badu vs. Jill Scott. We did not ask for these battles, but as they unfolded, we knew how much we needed this space, now more than ever.

The Erykah Badu vs. Jill Scott and Gladys Knight vs. Patti LaBelle were essential not just in the Verzuz series but also a world in turmoil. During no other time could so many Black folk tune in to celebrate Black womanhood within the culture. You could sense, from the comments in both events and the reactions on Twitter, that these four women staged a beautiful and well-needed intervention during a global pandemic. When the consumption of Black suffering is all around, seeing Black folk come together in celebration always feels good. Joy in Sorrow.

REFERENCES

Allaire, C. (2020, May 10). Erykah Badu and Jill Scott's Instagram battle had fans shook. *Vogue*. https://www.vogue.com/article/erykah-badu-jill-scott-instagram-battle-stream

Brock, A. (2012). From the Blackhand side: Twitter as a cultural conversation. *Journal of Broadcasting & Electronic Media*, 56(4), 529–549.

Doaks, C. (2020, June 24). Erykah Badu and Jill Scott love each other to life in first women's Verzuz battle. *Ms*. https://msmagazine.com/2020/05/11/erykah-badu-and-jill-scott-love-each-other-to-life-in-first-womens-verzuz-battle

Duthely, R. (2017). Black feminist hip-hop rhetorics and the digital public sphere. *Changing English: Studies in Cultural Education*, 24(2), 202–212.

Everett, A. (2002). The revolution will be digitized: Afrocentricity and the digital public sphere. *Social Text*, 20(2), 125–146.

France, L. R. (2020, September 14). Gladys Knight and Patti LaBelle gave us legendary Verzuz battle. *CNN Entertainment*. https://www.cnn.com/2020/09/14/entertainment/gladys-knight-patti-labelle-verzuz/index.html

Goins, M. (2011). Playing with dialectics: Black female friendship groups as a homeplace. *Communication Studies*, *62*(5), 531–546.

Graham, R., & Smith, S. (2016). The content of our #characters: Black Twitter as counterpublic. *Sociology of Race and Ethnicity*, *2*(4), 433–449.

Gunn, T. (2020, September 22). Patti LaBelle and Gladys Knight broke personal streaming record after Verzuz battle. *REVOLT*. https://www.revolt.tv/news/2020/9/22/21451546/gladys-knight-patti-labelle-streaming-verzuz

hooks, b. (1986). Sisterhood: Political solidarity between women. *Feminist Review*, *23*, 125–138.

Kendall, M. (2020, September 14). The Patti LaBelle vs. Gladys Knight "Verzuz" was made special by the music and our memories. *NBC News*. https://www.nbcnews.com/think/opinion/patti-labelle-vs-gladys-knight-verzuz-was-made-special-music-ncna1240073

Kernodle, T. (2014). Black women working together: Jazz, gender, and the politics of validation. *Black Music Research Journal*, *34*(1), 27–55.

Knight, G., LaBelle, P., & Warwick, D. (n.d.). Sisters In The Name of Love. *YouTube*. https://www.youtube.com/watch?v=lW4OUbS7RCQ

Lindsey, T. (2013). If you look in my life: Love, hip-hop soul, and contemporary African American womanhood. *African American Review*, *46*(1), 87–99.

Mahon, M. (2020). *Black diamond queens: African American women and rock and roll*. Duke University Press.

McIver, J. (2002). *Erykah Badu: The first lady of Neo-Soul*. Sanctuary.

Neal, M. A. (2020, November 30). Patti LaBelle, the Doyenne of Philadelphia Soul. *The New York Times*. https://www.nytimes.com/2020/11/30/t-magazine/patti-labelle-philadelphia-soul.html

Oyeniyi, D. (2020, May 12). Erykah Badu and Jill Scott's Verzuz battle felt more intimate than a live show. *Texas Monthly*. https://www.texasmonthly.com/the-culture/erykah-badu-jill-scott-verzuz-instagram-battle/

Pough, G. D. (2004). *Check it while I wreck it: Black womanhood, hip-hop culture, and the public sphere*. Northeastern University Press.

Pryor, B., & Outley, C. (2021). "Last Night a DJ Saved My Life": @Dnice #ClubQuarantine: Digitally Mediating Ritualistic Leisure Spaces During Isolation. *Leisure Sciences: An Interdisciplinary Journal*, *43* (1–2), 330–342.

Salaam, K. Y. (1995). It didn't jes grew: The social and aesthetic significance of African American music, *29*(2), 351–375.

Seymour, C. (2020, September 11). *"Superwoman": Gladys Knight, Patti LaBelle, and Dionne Warwick's Rare Collab*. Udiscovermusic.

Smitherman, G. (2006). *Word from the Mother: Language and African Americans*. Routledge.

Yarbrough, M., & Bennett, C. (2000). Cassandra and the Sistahs: The peculiar treatment of African American women in the myth of women as liars. *Journal of Gender, Race and Justice*, *3*(2), 625–658.

Chapter 3

Don't Take it Personal

Perceptions of Envy, Competitiveness, and Authenticity in the Brandy v. Monica Verzuz Battle

Aisha Damali Lockridge and Janée N. Burkhalter

In Spring 2020, Timothy "Timbaland" Mosely and Kasseem "Swizz Beatz" Dean created Verzuz, a free social media event series that invites the audience to come for both the music and the drama. Created in a fit of what feels like bored desperation, Verzuz becomes an opportunity to strengthen communal bonds. The event series grants participants more opportunities to model cultural and social creation that live on as maps for future generations (Dotson, 2013). Building on a tradition of artistic collaboration and long-standing rivalry, Verzuz positions itself as a labor of Black love from its creators to its quarantined audience, and yet, the chance for a music lovefest is not the greatest gift Verzuz provides its audience. That present comes packaged as an opportunity to let go of respectability politics. Rather than insisting that its audience watch respectable Black people do respectable Black things, Verzuz invites viewers to a no-holds-barred battle. This is particularly remarkable because this planned face-off is atypical of most public rivalries between women; "when it comes to women, competitiveness and rivalry have been objects of long-standing moral and social disapproval, even in capitalist and democratic societies in which competitiveness in general is greatly valued" (Ngai, 2006, p. 109 emphasis hers). Interested in not merely bearing witness to envy and competitiveness, we examine the Brandy Norwood and Monica Arnold Verzuz battle (Verzuz TV, 2020a) to reveal the critical potential of these mechanisms. That is, what do envy and competitiveness do, reflect, reveal? Verzuz rejects respectability and in so doing allows the women who perform there to be free of controlling images like the Black lady (Collins, 1995, 2001). We are invited down to the Verzuz to see a truly rare thing: a sanctioned battle royale between women; there is something deeply Black and deeply feminist about such an invitation.

VERZUZ

Known as "one of the music industry's most notable quarantine offerings" (Millman, 2020), Verzuz is an online music event series created by music producers Swizz Beatz and Timbaland in the midst of the COVID-19 pandemic. One night in March 2020, Timbaland shared some posts to his Instagram (IG) account talking about music he was working on and eventually asked Swizz Beatz, "Where you at?!" Within twenty-four hours, the two came together via Instagram Live (IG Live) for a five-hour matchup playing music from their devices and telling stories in between (Kennedy, 2020). This was not their first matchup, however.

After performing in the 2018 Hot 97 Summer Jam battle, the two began talks to take the battle on tour. Their original idea was for the producers' tour to visit different cities and invite singers and rappers to join them, performing the songs the two had previously produced. But as COVID-19 spread across the world resulting in massive sickness, death, and quarantines, the idea was put on hold until their unannounced IG Live battle drew over 20,000 viewers. This unexpected reception sparked another way to move their idea forward. Leveraging the success of their IG Live, the two began reaching out to producers, singers, rappers, and songwriters in their networks, inviting them to battle via Instagram. The artist would each select a song from their catalogue and go round-for-round with an industry peer. This back-and-forth format is common within Hip-Hop whether the battle is between rappers, DJs, or breakdancers (LaBoskey, 2001). Bragging, boasting, and trash talking are common in battling as ways to engender a response from a competitor (LaBoskey, 2001), display confidence and establish dominance. Traditionally, winners are determined based on some combination of creativity, content, delivery, and crowd response (Sawyer III, 2015). Though Verzuz does not designate either artist as the official winner at the end of the event, viewers and industry outlets and even the event's creators have at times taken it upon themselves to score each round and declare a winner (Jenkins, 2020; Lamarre, 2020).

Unlike that initial IG Live which took the form of friendly competition (Jenkins, 2020) during which Timbaland and Swizz Beatz celebrated their own accomplishments as well as one another's and the artists with which they worked, several of the early exchanges felt more like combat. For example, during an April 2020 battle, Mannie Fresh and Scott Storch took several jabs at one another fueled by Fresh's jokes and even skits about Storch's drug addiction and legal problems (Kennedy, 2020; Marie, 2020). This negativity turned off many potential performers and spurred the creators to reframe the event as a celebration of their contributions to music (Kennedy, 2020). This reframing helped Timbaland and Swizz Beatz recruit even more participants including stars from the R&B, Neo-Soul, and Soul genres—including contemporaries Brandy and Monica. As Brandy told Kennedy (2020), "We wanted it to be a celebration, because people have really put us against each other in so many different ways. We had a very controversial song. There was real beef at one point between us, and we just didn't want that to be the highlight of what the Verzuz was. Once we were sure that that wasn't going to be the case—and we were really going to be able to come together and celebrate each other—that was the tipping point." The stated intentions of all involved seem to be above board but below the surface the history makes it difficult to see a way to this rosy end.

BRANDY V. MONICA: THE BOY IS MINE

Brandy, a mezzo soprano, was born in Mississippi and raised in California. She signed a record deal at the age of fourteen and her debut album, *Brandy*, was released in 1994. Brandy released her seventh studio album, *B7*, in 2020. She has also starred in television shows such as *Moesha* (1996–2001) and *The Game* (2012–2015) as well as the 1997 TV movie, *Cinderella*.

Monica, a soprano, was born and raised in Georgia. She signed a record deal at the age of twelve and released her debut album, *Miss Thang,* in 1995 at the age of fourteen. Monica is the youngest female artist ever to have two #1 back-to-back hits on Billboard's R&B chart, both originating from her debut album. She has also appeared on various television shows including *Living Single* (1996) and *90210* (1999) as well as films such as *Pastor Brown* (2009). She released her eighth studio album, *Code Red*, in 2015.

Both artists, over the course of their careers, will enact Diva antics not just for attention but also in an attempt to direct their lives and livelihoods away from stale, industry narratives of unremarkable, unthinking petty rivalry (Lockridge, 2012). The idea of the Diva has always summoned a tension. Diva, etymologically, has a long history with its first attribution describing a beautiful but untalented woman who is cast in what was then a typical role for men or castrati (Lockridge, 2012). With so much pressure and possibility buried in its meaning and usage, we meet the Diva in the twenty-first century, largely, as a title bestowed upon greatness. No one is gauche enough to legitimately claim the title for herself, rather, like a knighthood, one becomes a Diva after trials, after demonstrations of excellence, often with a dash of bad behavior added for flavor.

Early in her career, Brandy was called a "diva-in-training" (Lister, 2001) and mentioned with the likes of Prima Divas such as Whitney Houston and Mariah Carey; however, similar claims have not been made about Monica. Lister argues that Prima Divas are known for their indisputable "vocal chops" (Lister, 2001, p. 2) and recognized for a "sheer vocal talent [which] cannot be disputed regardless of whether you love her or hate her." Designated early as having such chops, Brandy, sometimes referred to by her nickname "The Vocal Bible" (Ford, 2020), is highly critical of her own singing talent throughout her Verzuz battle with Monica. Brandy narrates struggle and lack during the event, even arguing when Monica celebrates her opponent's talent. For example, in round five after showcasing "Baby," Brandy verbally tussles with Monica over her technique:

Brandy: "God fell asleep on my false[tto]."
Monica: "Why you say that?"
Brandy: "Because my falsetto only goes to a certain place and then ... but I make up for it in other ways."
Monica: "I disagree."
Brandy: "You go right 'head on and disagree."
Monica: "I think we all hard on ourselves about certain stuff."
Brandy: "Mo, my false[tto] stops at a certain point. Okay."
Monica: "It really doesn't though. You got records that say otherwise."
Brandy: "Don't challenge me on that."
Monica: "Okay then."
Brandy: "Your turn."

While Brandy performs the role of a hypercritical diva throughout the battle, Monica affects the sense of a cultural one. After a terrible fashion choice in her 1995 video "Before You Walk Out of My Life," which still generates memes even now, Monica has developed a sleek signature style and a taste for Fendi. Unlike Brandy, Monica often has been labelmates with uncontested Divas such as Whitney Houston and worked under the direction of queenmaker, Clive Davis. Maybe never called a Diva herself beyond the popular press, Monica, routinely, has been in their midst and she acts like it. Publicly she is never critical of her singing and often claims to record songs in a single take as we highlight later.

Verzuz hit a new milestone when over six million people tuned in across Instagram and Apple Music to watch Brandy and Monica battle on August 31, 2020 (Kennedy, 2020). This battle was a long time in the making as the women had not been in the same room in eight years. While any number of factors such as the need to escape the reality of the COVID-19 pandemic or desire to connect with others may have drawn over one million viewers, research in media and communications also suggests that the desire to witness competition and a draw toward vengeance and voyeurism may have also helped Verzuz reach a milestone with this particular battle (Aslama & Pantti, 2006; Lundy, Ruth & Park, 2008; Reiss & Wiltz, 2004). These contemporaries debuted in the late 1990s and have been compared for decades. In fact, in a 1998 interview Monica is quoted as saying, "It's ironic that Brandy and I came out at the same time. We knew the comparisons would be huge but not all the talk about us being at each other's throats. That really bothered both of us because it made us look petty and we aren't" (Chambers & Samuels, 1998). The public duel between Brandy and Monica began over two decades ago and despite their protestations, many attribute their rivalry to their shared number-one duet "The Boy is Mine." It makes sense that folks would make this attribution given that the song's subject is a competition. Released to both acclaim and melodrama the song centers two women vying for the affection of the same man. "The Boy is Mine" begins with an idea and a rumor. Brandy and Rodney "Darkchild" Jerkins penned the song which was originally recorded as a solo that didn't quite pop. The two writers reconceptualized the song as a competition; "we didn't want to do a regular duet as if they were best buds or in high school or something. We should do something that makes them kind of competitive" (Tanzer, 2018). Hoping to capitalize on the young artists' perceived mutual disdain for the other, managers and studios ironed out a deal to record the song for Darkchild Productions at Atlantic. Definitive information about the recording sessions is scant but what we do know is that a song originally written by and attributed to Brandy and Darkchild eventually gains an additional producer, Dallas Austin. Dallas's entry likely comes by way of Monica. He signed Monica and served as executive producer on her first album under his Arista imprint, Rowdy Records. Each producer, in later years will offer up details of jealousy and violence. The artists say much less. Beyond subtle jabs on social media and during live performances, Brandy says little about her interactions with Monica during the making of "The Boy is Mine." Monica eventually offers more concretely "we could barely stay in the room with each other. By no means was it jealousy or envy. She and I are polar opposites" (Julious, 2018). Even this bare insight was missing in 1998. Instead, at the time, the stars' management teams released a joint statement admonishing the media for creating a false narrative about Brandy and Monica's imaginary rivalry. It read in part, "they did interviews together, had their picture taken together, had adjoining dressing rooms [. . .] and prayed together prior to going onstage to perform. Clearly, there are certain individuals who are trying to create a rift between Brandy and Monica. Such ongoing negativity is totally unfair to these two gifted teenagers, both of whom are simply working hard to build successful careers in a very tough business" (Yahoo! Music Backstage, 1998).

It might have all been just a smart marketing plan that built on a patriarchal, misogynist discourse of catty, competitive women but somewhere along the way it seems to have gotten real as both artists and camps attempt to leverage the song's success as belonging to one artist or another. The single "The Boy is Mine" is released in May 1998 as the lead single for Brandy's June 1998 album, *Never Say Never*. At Arista, Monica's second album is entitled "The Boy is Mine" and released in July of the same year. Austin explains the decision to name the album after the duet: "we wanted to reflect that it was a duet, not just a song on Brandy's album featuring Monica" (Gardner, 1998). It seems important to note here that Monica does not have a writing or producing credit on the song. While each camp explicitly defines the song as a duet, each attempts to stake ownership in its success and understandably so. The song spent twenty-seven weeks on the Billboard Hot 100 hitting #1 on June 6, 1998. It is the first #1 single for both artists, becomes the best-selling single of 1998 and goes on to win a Grammy for Best R&B Vocal Performance by a Duo or Group (*Billboard*). It will be the only Grammy either wins in their careers though there are several more nominations for each in the years that follow. Given this, the envy and competitiveness between these two artists seems prophetic. While the media attention around "The Boy is Mine" wanes and the two record another duet, "It All Belongs to Me" in 2012, the artists' animosities are not abated. During her Essence Fest 2018 performance, Brandy changes the lyrics from "the boy is mine" to "the song is mine". As the performance draws to an end she states emphatically while beating her chest "I gotta claim what's mine. If I don't got the boy, I got the song. You know what I'm saying" (The Shade Room, 2018). An adoring crowd erupts in support even more enthusiastic than during the previous singalong; it is hard to imagine the audience isn't here hoping to see just a little shade thrown. They are not disappointed. That same day Monica posts a picture of herself on Instagram dressed in all Black with a T-shirt reading "Get the Strap" posed with two Draco semiautomatic pistols, one pointed at the camera. The caption mentions neither Brandy nor her performance and yet the message is clear. A rivalry exists and though decades old, burns.

Even before the Verzuz took place, the event's producers found a way to leverage the melodrama surrounding "They Boy is Mine" by creating a commercial promoting the battle. It begins with Mekhi Phifer who played the boy of the song's title, now married and making plans with his wife, apparently having chosen neither Brandy nor Monica for his life partner. His phone lights up with first a call from Monica and then one from Brandy. He rejects both calls proclaiming his faithfulness to his wife and his determination to tune into the scheduled Verzuz. Playful and fun, the ad, while playing faded bits of the original video, enlivens nostalgia for a specific era, type of music, even type of beef. By referencing that 1998, fictitious battle Verzuz tells us, collectively, to come for the music memories with a wink and nod to the fallout surrounding "The Boy is Mine." The fallout, though, is not insignificant. Verzuz capitalizes on what appears to be melodrama by bringing the two together in a public forum and inviting us to participate in their presumed contentious reunion. This is not how rivalries between women are generally expected or even permitted to play out (Ngai, 2005, 2006). So they attempt to perform as they always have: Brandy, performing the role of the good girl next door, and Monica performing as a refined "Goonica." In spite of their performances, the audience is primed to witness a competitive battle royale.

WOMEN IN THE MUSIC INDUSTRY: ENVY, COMPETITIVENESS, AND AUTHENTICITY

Limiting the rivalry between Brandy and Monica to simple pettiness undermines their serious goals of success. Each is attempting to stake her claim in the music industry and likely, achieve full-fledged Diva status. Achievement in the music industry has come to be evaluated in a variety of quantitative and qualitative ways. Quantitative measures may include metrics such as the number of concert-goers, the number of streams or the amount of social media chatter. Qualitative measures may include one's ability to collaborate or to appear authentic. These qualitative measures may be of pertinent relevance to Black women musicians. In some cases, success may be defined by sisterhood (Emerson, 2002) as women artists collaborate and build community particularly as a way to remain competitive in a male-dominated industry. As Brandy notes, "For us to come together and to be this powerful together, it just spoke volumes as women, as Black women coming together. I felt like we really were able to seize the moment, and I think it was a sign that we should work together more. We should do more things together. And not to take away from what we do individually, because she's a force all by herself, but it's something about when we come together. I wanted her to feel that, and I just wanted her to feel celebrated from me" (Kennedy, 2020).

During the Brandy and Monica Verzuz, each artist sprinkled vocal collaborations throughout their battle; Brandy played five and Monica six. The majority of these collaborations were with male singers or rappers. Brandy's "I Wanna Be Down (remix)" and "Missing You" stand out because they feature female collaborations with notable female artists such as Queen Latifah (Monica's former manager) and Gladys Knight, respectively. With fewer collaborations overall and even fewer with women, before playing "Trust," a Keyshia Cole song on which she is featured, Monica says, "collaborative efforts are really super special to me." In a battle meant to showcase their own talents, the decision to spend a third of that time on collaborations is striking. This emphasis on collaboration suggests the seriousness with which they treat their careers.

The two do not limit their collaborations to just vocal collaborations, as each artist highlighted the range of producers and songwriters with whom they have worked. This, at times, serves as a source of tension between Brandy and Monica. For example, when introducing "Everything to Me" during the first round, Monica says she collaborated on the song "with two people we both love—Missy [Elliot] and Jazmine [Sullivan]." To which Brandy responds to a confused Monica, "Well first of all, why y'all ain't call me for that?" Another awkward moment arises during the sixteenth round as Brandy sets up her song "Sitting Up in My Room." The song appears on the *Waiting to Exhale* soundtrack, an album produced by Kenny "Babyface" Edmonds, which notably features only female singers. As Brandy tells her story, Monica interrupts to say, "They left me out of that. They ain't call me for that." Brandy apologizes saying Monica was left out because she was a newer artist and that "Don't Take it Personal" had just been released. Despite the awkward misplaced apology, Brandy goes on to brag that "all my idols was on that album" [*sic*] and that Notorious B.I.G. gave her a shout out in one of his songs because of "Sitting Up in My Room." As they narrativize how and with whom they have collaborated, they attempt to show their prestige while also demonstrating their collegiality.

While women's success in music is often attributed to collaboration, Black women's success has also centered opposition. There have been notable rivalries between Black women artists: Diana Ross and Mary Wilson, Mariah Carey and Whitney Houston, Lil' Kim and Foxy Brown, Nikki Minaj and Remy Ma. Competitiveness and an inability to get along with others are central mythologies about Black women in music. By way of example, this varies significantly from the ways men in jazz are encouraged to be competitive. Competitiveness is believed to help men distill their voices and become more creative. Women, instead, are "forced into battle to be the 'one' female creative voice that survives and earns a place in the historical narrative" (Kernodle, 2014, pp. 28–29).

Unlike the sentimental Mekhi Phifer advertisement, the audience likely enters the Verzuz with a distinct favorite because we have been encouraged to do this—to decide who is "the one." And yet the reframing of these events argues that Verzuz attempts to do the opposite. Swizz Beatz says the ultimate goals are love and reconciliation. "[*Verzuz*] showed a lot of the youth and a lot of the musicians who are going [through] problems or have problems with other musicians . . . that the ending can be something that's celebrated in positivity" (Tyrell, 2020). This runs counter to the promotional material that mimics that of a prize fight. Placards of each musician's song stats are created in advance of battles and presented via social media. Glossy commercials featuring battle drawn artists are released by sponsors like Ciroc. Eventually, meme culture takes over. In spite of claims otherwise, Verzuz is a competitive match because Verzuz makes it one. By definition, two artists are pitted against each other and implicitly, we are invited to choose a winner. This runs not just counter to the messaging of love and reconciliation the creators issue but seems to evoke the double-voiced nature of Black speech (Gates, 1998). When Verzuz posts "You brought joy at a much-needed time" (Verzuz TV, 2020b) we must acknowledge the multivalent nature of that joy. It is not all peace and reconciliation; it is also the joy of watching adversarial foes do battle (Reiss & Wiltz, 2004). Verzuz battles are not live music events. At best, they are musical events where live music or something else may spontaneously occur. We argue here, largely, the audience is here to see that something else. Every step along the way the audience has been encouraged to predecide a winner. So if the needle can be moved at all, the audience must look at what is available to see and judge—affect: styling, positionality, engagement. That is: Who seems real? Who's still got it?

Brandy's and Monica's competitiveness certainly comes through during the Verzuz battle as the two highlight times when they were left out of potential collaborations. It also surfaces as Brandy challenges Monica's statements about some of her earliest tracks. One striking example occurs at the end of round five when the two discuss Monica's song "Like This and Like That" from her debut album *Miss Thang*. Notably, this exchange happens at the end of the same round during which Monica compliments Brandy's vocal range and talks about Brandy being hard on herself; within minutes of highlighting Brandy's talent, Monica is made to defend her own:

Brandy: "You were 12 when you did 'Like This and Like That'?!"
Monica: "Yeah. Yeah. Yeah. That was from the early batch of records. The record dropped . . . when, when everything came out I was thirteen."
Brandy: "Put that on everything?"
Monica: "On my daughter and sons . . . Yeah. So I recorded 'Like This and Like That' at 12."

Later, at the end of round twelve, Brandy expresses disbelief again; this time about Monica's recording style. After Brandy talks about her need to be perfect and says, "I may do a song 32 times," Monica responds, "Some of my greatest records are sing downs. One take. I start from the beginning, sing it down and don't touch it. Leave it." To which Brandy responds, "Girl, you better than me . . . One two sing-down. What?" We see in these exchanges another sort of competition—a competition about technique and outcomes. That is, what makes for a more successful artist: practice or natural talent? Each answers differently. Brandy seems to suggest in her queries that practice and perfection are required while Monica's flippant responses suggest the opposite. In this we can arguably see the underbody of their public duel. "The Boy is Mine" is what fans see above ground, but there are deeper questions about which these artists rangle when we take the time to look.

Unlike the Ashanti and Keyshia Cole Verzuz, where arguably the artists affect a similar visual aesthetic, the differences between Brandy and Monica's affect is stark and revealing. Brandy dressed in a tapestry coat, unremarkable blue jeans, and faux locs affects the persona of a stylishly clad high school teacher armed with poems and admonishments. Monica dressed in a Fendi logoed custom creation affects the persona of a chic model turned mom and spoke to the *sturm und drang* of romantic relationships. As the audience watches this battle, the differences between the musicians, differences which have always been present, become more obvious in the absence of live music. It makes more significant Monica's seeming disbelief that she and Brandy would be compared so continually and unfavorably (Chambers & Samuels, 1998). For the most part, Monica's affect makes her seem disinterested in the events at hand. Mostly, she talks to her off-screen guests and sways on occasion to a Brandy song or two. She is most animated, most engaged when she acts as her own personal song historian or when she is singing her most lovelorn songs. Brandy is ever engaged, sings along to her songs and parts of Monica's songs. She is less song historian and more self-critic. Outlining how difficult a song was to sing, how many times she didn't get a note correct. On the few occasions Monica admonishes herself, it is never about her voice, her singing, and her songs, it is about her reputation as a pugilistic lover. When Brandy attempts to home in on one such story, to make herself Monica's villain, Monica interrupts the insertion frankly: "What had happened was, we had a disagreement. That's that's what happened. We had a disagreement ... You know I only kick in doors if it's something involving the opposite sex." Brandy apologizes, somewhat chastened. Monica returns to her story and soon thereafter chart topper "So Gone" plays. In this exchange, we see envy at work. Brandy's stories, largely, feature self-doubt, whereas Monica's feature romance run amok. Perhaps envious of the seeming accessibility such stories might have to a social media audience, Brandy attempts to make herself a part of Monica's story. We see clearly then that envy operates here not as a subject in itself but as a "subject's affective response to a perceived inequality" (Ngai, 2005, p. 126). Brandy wants to seem as interesting, to have as much of the storytelling spotlight as her opponent. The envy she displays attempts to right a perceived injustice.

Beyond revisionist history, Brandy attempts to establish herself not only as the more serious singer, but the artist with the moral high ground. She leans on a politics of respectability to do so, but this is difficult in the Verzuz sphere because Verzuz is not rooted in that way and because Monica has not displayed an interest in that type of performance. In fact, Monica's relative lack of affect makes it difficult to divine anything about a potential internal monologue. That is, until she decides to play the song "Sideline Ho." Citing City Girls, Monica offers up the song as a moment of authenticity for "girls that's like me." As the song plays, in her most animated performance of the evening, Monica rises from her chair, squats, bops, mouths many of the lyrics, all while staring directly into the camera. The audience is invited into the song's narrative with each punctuated movement. The lyrics pose a series of questions; in call and response style, the audience is invited to respond:

> Do you got benefits? (No) Credit cards? (No) House keys? (No)
> Then you's a sideline ho
> Do you get pillow talk? (No) Held at night? (No)
> If you don't make his breakfast, you's a sideline ho (Arnold, 2007)

Throughout Monica's enthusiastic performance, a different kind of performance is taking place. As the first line of the song issues forth: "Ho, ho, sideline ho," Brandy covers her mouth in shock while telling her eighteenth-year-old daughter to cover her ears. She refuses to join in on the call and response portions of the song and uncharacteristically for this event, does not dance in her seat. In the aftermath of the performance, while claiming a lack of familiarity with City Girls, a Miami rap duo known for racy lyrics and a pugilistic spirit, Brandy entreats a very animated Monica with "my daughter is watching" and offers a lyric revision: "why couldn't it have been sideline—?" Brandy first refuses to say the word "ho" and then does so only as a seeming artistic experiment. At most, Brandy is willing to meet the word "ho" as an artist. As a musician Brandy begins to harmonize with Monica's singing of the word "ho." Monica is interested in the emotion and the story behind the song. Brandy is concerned with the lack of decorum the song displays and insists that even if they must continue discussing the song that they, at least stop saying the word. Monica replies by singing the word yet again. Each exchange throughout the battle highlights their differences as artists and forces the audience to further query the insistence that there be only one.

Authenticity has been integral to Verzuz, giving fans the opportunity to see the artists interact while learning the stories behind the songs. Authenticity is also considered an important key to success in music. While critical and ever sought after, authenticity is not something an artist can define for their listeners; rather, authenticity is ascribed by an audience to an artist. It is through the artists' narrations and performances that Verzuz viewers gain insight into the performer's point of view and from it determine authenticity. Largely, listeners believe that musicians only create and perform music that represents who they truthfully are (Bicknell, 2005;

Hargreaves et al., 2002; Meyer, 1961; Moore, 2002). So in addition to following artists via social media or watching their music videos (Burkhalter et al., 2017), fans also listen to songs seeking revealing personal details about the artists and use all of these revelations to ascribe authenticity (Redhead & Street, 1989). Both women reveal personal details and stories throughout the battle, presumably in the hopes of projecting authenticity. During the third round, after playing the song "So Gone," Monica shares, "I've been on my best behavior the last few years but there was a time I was kicking in doors and smacking down chicks," just as she sings in the third verse. Though Monica is not a writer on that song, she highlights the fact that the lyrics are still true to her personal experience. Later, during the fifth round, while reminiscing about *Miss Thang* Monica shares "the goal for Dallas was really just for me to be me . . . So he took my attitude about things and made a record," highlighting that she has been her authentic self since coming onto the music scene more than twenty years ago. This revelation was likely read as authentic to the audience. It revealed something about the nature of Monica's studio sessions that seemed to match the subjects of the songs she sings most often.

Authentic music must also be delivered through honest, expressive performance (Mayhew, 1999). While expectations of authenticity exist for all musicians, there is an added layer female singers must manage as "the voice is a place where identity can be projected" (Mayhew, 1999, p. 72). Throughout the Verzuz, then, it makes sense that both women talk about projecting their emotions through their music. For example, at the end of round twelve, Brandy says to Monica, "I love that you feel everything you, you sing and I do, too, but I do be . . . I'm such a perfectionist I [am] so worried . . . about the vocals being right and sometimes I forget [about] the feeling so thank you for reminding me of that today. I need to really do that a lot more. Even though I feel everything that I sing I do get caught up in the precision."

Finally, as authenticity is something that is perceived by another, it is notable that the two not only make claims of their own authenticity but also ascribe it to one another. After Brandy plays her track "He Is" to start round two, Monica focuses on Brandy's tone, "But the way you sang it, your tone is unmatched. But I always say that though. All jokes aside, straight up [your] tone is unmatched." And soon after, in response to Monica playing "Don't Take it Personal" in round four, Brandy notes how Monica's character shone through her performance. She cites Monica's passion and confidence as the very reasons she sought out the opportunity to record with her. "It became like a dream to do a song with you." It's ironic that authenticity is not only what drew Brandy to Monica but also the source of several awkward exchanges throughout the battle.

ACTS OF INHERITANCE

Verzuz identifies a new orientation toward Black feminist cultural production and thus serves as an act of inheritance. This new orientation undoes the idea that women, and particularly Black women, must be "an unusually exemplary example" (Ngai, 2005, p. 149). Neither Brandy nor Monica presents a prototypical good example. We are invited instead to revel in their competitiveness and their envy. It is easy to imagine that the Brandy and Monica rivalry is tied up in an "ongoing debate concerning the relationship between 'wanting to be' and 'wanting to have'" (Ngai, 2005, p. 139). This oversimplification limits our ability to read nuance in their interactions and most importantly, limits how we are able to appreciate their acts of inheritance. That is, how are they projecting themselves into the future? What are they modeling for the folks that come after them? (Dotson, 2013) Bernice Johnson Reagon argues that "the only way you can take yourself seriously is if you can throw yourself into the next period beyond your little meager human-body-mouth-talking all the time" (Reagon, 1983, p. 365). This suggestion allows us to easily hold space for the idea that while each artist experiences a sense of both wanting to have [the level of fame, attention, adoration] and wanting to be [figuratively inhabit the space] for the other, they are still revealing, modeling, outlining other ways of being Black women artists outside of the confines in which they must operate. In short, these are serious artists who take their artistry seriously, even as they reveal it differently. We witness it in their demeanor, their narratization, their studied ensembles, and their desire to be recognized as separate entities. It is not pettiness for its own sake. It is two artists attempting to demarcate productive difference. It is restorative. The battle to be "the one" leads to the exclusion of other women. Brandy and Monica are highlighting their difference so as to claim unique space in an industry that insists on sameness. Monica notes, "I have so desperately wanted to put to bed the unnecessary comparisons—the idea that you have to choose one. I feel like Brandy is one of the greatest of all time . . . And I, too, paved a way for myself with a very different sense of motivation, coming from a very different place" (Kennedy, 2020).

Arguably, Brandy and Monica have hits, net worths in a similar range, and name recognition, their perceived audiences and relevancy have shifted over time and arguably in different directions. So what are they hurling into the future? "Envy's critical potential thus resides in its ability to highlight a refusal to idealize quality X, even an ability to attack its potential for idealization by transforming X into something nonsingular and replicable, while at the same time enabling acknowledgment of its culturally imposed desirability" (Ngai, 2006, pp. 161–162). By way of example, we can observe easily the imposition of cultural desirability for sameness in the Ashanti and

Keyshia Cole Verzuz. Their Verzuz battle returns to the original format with both artists performing from separate locations. In spite of this it feels as though they have employed the same stylist. Both are dressed in Black taffeta gowns, both wear dresses highlighting cleavage, both have long straightened hair styled with a side part, both employ similar makeup palettes. They have been transformed into something nonsingular and replicable (Ngai, 2006, p. 162). This is not the case with Brandy and Monica. Instead, their interactions "highlight a refusal to idealize quality X" (Ngai, 2006, p. 161). Monica's Goonica persona does not morph into Brandy's good girl one and neither is ultimately idealized. Their mutual envy and competitiveness reveals an insistence on being regarded as individual artists. More specifically, we witness two artists attempting to self-define their success in an industry that insists that there can only be one success story. Their fear is a real one: "in the social context of racism and sexism [. . .] an emphasis on type automatically poses the threat of obscuring variation" (Ngai, 2006, p. 119). What may appear as petty artists throwing shade seems upon closer inspection more like artists fighting to be seen as themselves. The purpose and value of envy are often examined as the thing itself but mostly, it is a mechanism that creates an opportunity for critical inquiry. This inquiry reveals the patriarchal nature of a static music industry machine and the *schadenfreude* of its audience. Throughout their careers, both artists, while enjoying the early success of "The Boy is Mine" have done as much as they can to stamp out the rumors of jealousy and most importantly, to assert themselves as contemporaries but not members of the same artistic cohort. Maybe this time we will listen, but probably not.

REFERENCES

Arnold, M. (2007). Sideline Ho [Song]. On *The Makings of Me*. J Records.

Aslama, M., & Pantti, M. (2006). Talking alone: Reality TV, emotions and authenticity. *European Journal of Cultural Studies*, 9(2), 167–184.

Bicknell, J. (2005). Just a song? Exploring the aesthetics of popular song performance. *Journal of Aesthetics and Art Criticism*, 63(Summer), 261–270.

Burkhalter, J. N., Curasi, C. F., Thornton C. G., & Donthu, N. (2017). Music and its multitude of meanings: Exploring what makes brand placements in music videos authentic. *Journal of Brand Management*, 24(2), 140–160. https://doi.org/10.1057/s41262-017-0029-5

Chambers, V., & Samuels, A. (1998). Diva rising: Meet the other Monica. *Newsweek*, 132(4), 56.

Collins, P. H. (1991). *Black Feminist Thought*. New York: Routledge.

———. (2005). *Black Sexual Politics: African Americans, Gender, and New Racism*. New York: Routledge.

Dotson, K. (2013). Radical love: Black philosophy as deliberate acts of inheritance. *The Black Scholar*, 43(4), December, 38–45. https://doi.org/10.5816/blackscholar.43.4.0038

Emerson, R. A. (2002). Where my girls at? Negotiating black womanhood in music videos. *Gender & Society*, 16(1), 115–135. https://doi.org/10.1177/0891243202016001007

Ford, S. (2020, August 1). Brandy is still standing. *Entertainment Weekly*. https://ew.com/music/brandy-b7-interview/

Gates, H. L. (1989). *The Signifying Monkey*. Oxford: Oxford University Press.

Gardner, E. (1998, July 7). Next from the diva machine. *Los Angeles Times*. https://www.latimes.com/archives/la-xpm-1998-jul-07-ca-1304-story.html

Hargreaves, D. J., Miell, D., & MacDonald, R. A. R. (2002). What are musical identities, and why are they important? In: R. A. R. MacDonald, D. J. Hargreaves, & D. Miell (eds.) *Musical Identities*. New York: Oxford University Press, 1–20.

Jenkins, C. (2020, November 20). All the Verzuz battles ranked. *Vulture*. https://www.vulture.com/2020/11/verzuz-instagram-live-battles-ranked.html

Julious, B. (2018, February 28). "The Boy is Mine" is a radical song about choosing friendship over drama. *Vice*. https://www.vice.com/en/article/qvemjx/the-boy-is-mine-brandy-monica-friendship-over-rivalry

Kennedy, G. (2020, November 19). Inside the unstoppable rise of Verzuz. *GQ*. https://www.gq.com/story/verzuz-oral-history

Kernodle, T. L. (2014). Black women working together: Jazz, gender and the politics of validation. *Black Music Research Journal*, 34(1), 27–55. https://doi.org/10.5406/blacmusiresej.34.1.0027

LaBoskey, S. (2001). Getting off: Portrayals of masculinity in hip hop dance in film. *Dance Research Journal*, 33(2), 112–120. https://doi.org/10.2307/1477808

Lamarre, C. (2020, September 1). Brandy vs. Monica in 'Verzuz' Battle of R&B Titans: See Billboard's Scorecard & Winner for the Event. *Billboard*. https://www.billboard.com/articles/columns/hip-hop/9443137/brandy-monica-verzuz-battle-scorecard/

Lister, L. (2001). Divafication: The deification of modern female pop stars. *Popular Music and Society*, 25(3/4), 1–10. https://doi.org/10.1080/03007760108591796

Lockridge, A. D. (2012). *Tipping on a Tight Rope: Divas in African American Literature*. Peter Lang.

Lundy, L. K., Ruth, A. M., & Park, T. D. (2008). Simply irresistible: Reality TV consumption patterns. *Communication Quarterly*, 56(2), 208–225. https://doi.org/10.1080/01463370802026828

Marie, E. (2020, November 24) Mannie fresh rejects another 'Verzuz,' defends skits against Scott Storch, *HNHH*. https://www.hotnewhiphop.com/mannie-fresh-rejects-another-verzuz-defends-skits-against-scott-storch-news.121820.html

Mayhew, E. (1999). Women in popular music and the construction of 'authenticity.' *Journal of Interdisciplinary Gender Studies*, 4(1), 63–81.

Meyer, L. B. (1961). On rehearing music. *Journal of the American Musicological Society*, 14(2), 257–267. https://doi.org/10.2307/829760

Moore, A. (2002). Authenticity as authentication. *Popular Music*, 21(2), 209–223. https://doi.org/10.1017/S0261143002002131

Millman, E. (2020, July 20). 'Verzuz,' the livestreaming quarantine darling, partners with Apple music. *Rolling Stone*. https://www.rollingstone.com/pro/news/verzuz-partners-with-apple-music-1031271/

Ngai, S. (2005). *Ugly Feelings*. Cambridge, MA: Harvard University Press.

———. (2006). Competitiveness: From Sula to Tyra. *Women's Studies Quarterly*, 34(3/4), 107–139. https://www.jstor.org/stable/40003529

Reagon, B. J. (1983). Coalition politics: Turning the century. In Barbara Smith (ed.) *Home Girls: A Black Feminist Anthology*. New York: Kitchen Table Press, 356–368.

Redhead, S., & Street, J. (1989). Have I the right? Legitimacy, authenticity, and community in folk politics. *Popular Music*, 8(2), 177–184. https://www.jstor.org/stable/853467

Reiss, S., & Wiltz, J. (2004). Why people watch reality TV. *Media Psychology*, 6(4), 363–378. https://doi.org/10.1207/s1532785xmep0604_3

Sawyer III, D. C. (2015). Step your game up: Teaching sociology through the art of the hip-hop rap battle. *Humanity & Society*, 39(2), 224–235. https://doi.org/10.1177%2F0160597615574552

Tanzer, M. (2018, July 26). When Brandy and Monica's "The boy is mine" ran the world. *The Fader*. https://www.thefader.com/2018/07/19/brandy-monica-boy-is-mine-podcast

Terrell, D. (2020, August 4). Brandy is back after rediscovering herself. *The Undefeated*. https://theundefeated.com/features/brandy-is-back-after-rediscovering-herself/

The Shade Room [theshaderoom]. (2018, July 8). #PressPlay: Okay! #Brandy hit the stage at #EssenceFest and she made sure to let the crowd know "The Boy Is Mine," is her song via. @inquisitivecarter [Post]. https://www.instagram.com/p/Bk-yeo-Bo-m/

Tyrell, N. (2020, December 29). How "Verzuz" became the Way Artists Make Amends. *Okayplayer*. https://www.okayplayer.com/culture/verzuz-matches-beefs-feuds.html

Verzuz TV [@verzuztv] (2020a, August 31). Monica vs. Brandy [Video] Instagram. https://www.instagram.com/tv/CEk_6UCnLtY/

———. (2020b, August 31). Thank you QUEENS for such a legendary #VERZUZ! You brought joy at a much needed time. Tell us your favorite moments! @thomasleijgraaff [Post]. https://www.instagram.com/p/CElGDCFD3KC/

Yahoo! Music Backstage. (1998, September 16). Brandy and Monica "Held Hands and Prayed Together." https://archive.is/20130209221059/http://music.yahoo.com/monica/news/brandy-and-monica-held-hands-and-prayed-together--12032969#selection-731.0-731.50

Chapter 4

The Way We Were

How Black Women Created Space with Verzuz

Kirstin Cheers

The first female-led Verzuz event, featuring Jill Scott and Erykah Badu on May 9, 2020, reached over 700,000 viewers and 1 billion impressions (Verzuz, 2020) on Instagram, surpassing Babyface and the memeified Teddy Riley. In August, Brandy and Monica, the teenage singing sensations from the 1990s (who had Black girls singing off-key in the middle of their mother's living rooms), amassed over six million viewers (Verzuz, 2020) across Instagram and Apple Music. The event occurred after Swizz Beats and Timbaland partnered with Apple Music to bring more visibility to the livestreamed events and allow artists to avoid technical issues, bringing the artists to one decorated space that allowed for more significant production. The legendary Patti LaBelle and Gladys Knight came together one night in September, grossing over two million viewers (Verzuz, 2020) in what social media dubbed as "Auntiechella." Each pairing has seen a significant increase in music streams on platforms including Apple Music and Spotify after their respective Verzuz events (Verzuz, n.d.). Verzuz has allowed Black female artists to reconnect with faithful fans during the pandemic, which has suspended concerts and gatherings. These virtual concerts continue to reign as the most viewed livestreamed Verzuz "battles" to date.

At the onset of the pandemic, long-time producers Swizz Beats and Timbaland created a virtual space that allowed two producers, songwriters, or artists to duel with their best twenty hits on Instagram Live. Before Scott and Badu's event aired on May 9, 2020, nine male-led battles premiered. These events' ethos denoted friendly competition as onlookers fussed back and forth on social media about who had the better catalog. The viewership numbers increased and remained consistent during the male-led events. Creators and viewers thought the anticipated Babyface and Teddy Riley would break new ground until Riley's overproduction in his home prevented a smooth telecast and left viewers disappointed until their rescheduled event. However, when Swizz Beats and Timbaland started to include Black women, everything changed.

This chapter analyzes the rhetoric of the Verzuz battles that featured Black women. The female-led Verzuz events were more successful because Black women and Black female artists from the 1970s, 1980s, and 1990s have a vernacular that audiences of various demographics embrace and comprehend, especially during political and social uncertainty. Exploring the history of Black women's performances and their ability to attract large crowds, the first sections looks at two Black female performers from two separate generations, Marian Anderson and Beyoncé. Their most notable performances occur during eras of segregation and the Black Lives Matter movement, respectfully. This comparison is relevant to that of Black female artists' Verzuz appearances during the ongoing COVID-19 pandemic and racial uprisings during the Summer of 2020. Utilizing Sarah Florini's theorization of networked publics, Verzuz events distinguish between Black female artists' rhetoric within the counterpublic of a diverse crowd of a performance and an enclave between the Black female artist and Black female audience. This rhetoric is also apparent in the relationships between the two competitors during Verzuz events: Jill Scott and Erykah Badu; Patti LaBelle and Gladys Knight; and Monica and Brandy. I analyze how their parings participated in creating an enclave public for Black women viewers. These enclaves allowed Black women viewers to congregate and disconnect from the white and patriarchal hegemony that historically silences and reduces Black women and their experiences. Black women authored tweets during the livestreamed events provide evidence of how these events resonated with Black women and further examines how Black women vernacular consoles, comforts, and confronts Black women—a local community—as an audience.

THE HISTORY OF BLACK WOMEN PERFORMANCES DURING SOCIAL AND RACIAL CRISIS

Marian Anderson was the first Black singer to perform at the White House, and by 1939, she had the third highest concert box office draw in the United States. The Daughters of the American Revolution (DAR), sorority of white women founded in 1890 for female descendants of American Revolution soldiers, prevented Anderson from performing at Constitution Hall in

Washington, DC, a venue space in which they owned. As news of their antics circulated, then First Lady Eleanor Roosevelt resigned her membership with DAR. She then immediately arranged for Anderson to sing on the Lincoln Memorial's steps on Easter Sunday, April 9, 1939. Anderson drew a diverse crowd of 75,000 people, the largest gathering to assemble there since the Lindberg reception in 1927 (Stamberg, 2014). With tears in her eyes, she sang "Nobody Knows the Trouble I've Seen," and "America," changing the lyrics from "of thee, I sing" to "of thee, we sing" (Stamberg, 2014). In her autobiography, *My Lord, What a Morning*, Marian Anderson said, "I had become, whether I liked it or not, a symbol representing my people" about experiencing reservations about performing at the height of the DAR controversy (Anderson, 1956, as cited in Hobson, 2008, p. 443). Anderson embraced, even in controversy, the importance of standing as a representative of African Americans who suffered discrimination in a white supremacist country and era. Moreover, while she stood as a proxy, her choice to change the words of one of the country's beloved anthems was intended to reach more than Black people and Black women, but the white audience who benefited from white supremacy and saw her only as entertainment. Even her tears were political.

While contemporary Black female artists are often outranked by white men and white women grossing higher in concerts and tours, one woman remains to give them a run for their money when it comes to selling out stadiums—Beyoncé. In 2016, Beyoncé grossed over $256 million during "The Formation World Tour," which held forty-nine shows in the United States and other countries and her highest-grossing show according to Billboard (Waddell, 2016).

The tour began soon after Beyoncé dropped her highly acclaimed ode to Black women, Lemonade (2016), which highlights Black suffering at the hands of law enforcement and the rise of protests in the era of Black Lives Matter. During her shows, Queen Bey centered images of Black women, from her background singers and dancers as a montage of images from protests and people Black people killed by police violence. Her routines and sequences did not shy away from symbols attributed to Black liberation like the fist in the air, Black leather costumes and Black barrettes. To her Black audience, these symbols are empowering, resonate with "Black Power" rhetoric that originated during the Black Panther era. It was a political denouncement of police violence and the oppressive political institutions that marginalize and criminalize Black bodies to the hegemonic audience. She is fully inserting herself in the conversations that call out injustice and inequity toward Black people, especially Black women. Beyoncé is denouncing being a mere entertainer and evolving into an active participant in the movement for Black lives. As Janelle Hobson (2008) asserts, Marian Anderson and Beyoncé both "encapsulate a moment when Black women's singing instigated social protest" (Hobson, 2008, p. 1).

The ongoing global COVID-19 pandemic disproportionately impacted Black and Brown communities, another debilitating force—literally and figuratively—robbing communities of color of their breath. Some states began to enforce lockdowns, curfews, and mandatory mask ordinances, further forcing people to remain in their homes and limit, if not eliminate, going to nonessential workspaces, congregating in churches, and socializing with family and friends. The COVID-19 infection rates also revealed that Black people and communities of color were suffering significantly.

On April 6, 2020, hundreds of doctors from across the country signed a letter composed by the Lawyers' Committee for Civil Rights under Law (Williams, 2020). The letter requested the federal government to release COVID-19 infection and death rates, asserting the concealing of race and ethnicity data prevented health professionals from serving communities of color, a vulnerable demographic for illness and disease such as diabetes, heart disease, and HIV/AIDS. The Centers for Disease Control and Prevention (CDC) only began reporting national data on confirmed COVID-19 cases by race on April 17, 2020 (Artiga, 2020). As of April 20, 2020, thirty-three states and DC reported race and ethnicity data on COVID-19 infection and death rates. Black people accounted for 34 percent of confirmed cases, compared to only 13 percent of the total population.

Also, there was a presidential election underway, and Black people—especially Black women—were called to "save America" from itself [again]. Black women were expected to turn-out in large numbers for the Democratic candidate, Joe Biden, and his running mate, Kamala Harris. She would become the first Black, first South Asian and first woman elected as vice president of the United States. Donna Edwards (2019) penned in *The Washington Post*, "The numbers clearly show that the real juice for Democrats rests with women of color." "No candidate can ignore black women in the primary season and still hope to engage them after winning the party nomination—that won't fly" (Edwards, 2019).

Edwards explains that Black women voters were the Democratic Party's best bet at winning against Donald Trump and "reclaiming" the White House, Senate, and House of Representatives. Black women like Stacey Abrams and LaTosha Brown of Black Voters Matter led grassroots efforts in Georgia and across the country to register more Black voters and catapult them to the polls during early voting. The eagerness to elect the first Black woman to the vice presidency and painting the White House and Congress blue was not as exciting for everyone. "We are the first people to be abused, but also the ones expected to save democracy," said Stacy Cole-Bell, a Black woman and an Atlanta-based lawyer to the Atlanta Journal-Constitution (Suggs, 2020, para. 14).

Cole-Bell's words describe fatigue, a dismissal and abandonment from a system that simultaneously depended on Black women to mobilize those abused bodies to vote out Donald Trump.

Like Anderson's and Beyoncé's historic performances, Scott and Badu's Verzuz arrived at the right time: in a moment of a health crisis, political fatigue and, unfortunately, at the threshold of racial unrest. Black women are an unintentional remedy in political and social unrest. It means the vernacular of Black women (Black women vernacular) not only resonates with the local community (other Black women) but also translates to others, presenting as a source of comfort and guidance. From grandmothers, sisters, congress people, and pastors—Black women can reach audiences beyond their public and draw larger audiences, especially in times of turmoil when needed the most.

VERZUZ: A COUNTER PUBLIC FOR MANY, AND AN ENCLAVE FOR FEW

Expounding from Catherine Squires' theorization of counter publics and enclaves, Sarah Florini (2019, p. 70) introduces digital spaces as oscillating publics, which she defines as network publics that shift between counter publics and enclaves (2019, p. 72). Florini argues against the Habermasian concept that a public requires an "active deliberation and explicit political discussion." Instead, Florini adds that "for marginalized groups, seemingly mundane activities often come to take on political importance" (2019, p. 70). Using danah boyd's theorization, a networked public consists of two elements: "(1) the space constructed through networked technologies and (2) the imagined collective that emerges as a result of the intersection of people, technology, and practice." In this case, we can define Verzuz as a networked public. Verzuz's platform on Instagram (and later Apple Music and YouTube) contribute as networked technologies and the audiences, which span from Black Americans to other ethnicities and identities, opens the door for people to participate in the display of Black music. In Squires' definition, "counter-publics engage in debate with wider publics." However, enclaves can divide themselves from the larger population and center marginalized groups in discussions of politics, culture, and society.

The Verzuz network has the functionality to shift to and from a wider audience, afforded by Instagram, Apple Music, and YouTube, including non-Black people. Because of partnerships outside of Instagram and transitioning from artists streaming from their devices to meeting at a central location provided by Verzuz, the audience expands and welcomes new viewers. However, as those same artists begin to speak of their experiences, narratives, and backgrounds (professionally, musically, and personally), a boundary is erected. The wider audience can only observe but not participate. For Black women artists, that audience grows smaller and consists of an exclusive Black woman group.

Jill Scott vs. Erykah Badu.

These large numbers and broad viewership, from concerts to digital spaces, convey that Black female artists connect and communicate with a broad audience, especially in eras of oppression and global catastrophe. Since March 2020, COVID-19, alongside claiming the lives of millions, has pushed Americans into the confines of their homes, leaving many to cancel plans of travel and preventing any semblance of gathering with others. Schools, salons, restaurants, and churches closed (some did not depend on the size and state and local government mandates) before state and local governments enacted mask mandates and prohibiting congregating with people outside of those who live in the same home. Thus, when a flyer with the face of Betty Shabazz, the wife of Malcolm X, appeared on the Verzuz Instagram page with the words, "Jill Scott vs. Erykah Badu," there was a collective exhale. Melanie McFarland of Salon wrote in November:

> Early May is when the world first starting to press in on me. It became clear that this pandemic wasn't ending any time soon. I'd seen too many people flouting mask mandates, heard too many yard parties packed with loud people getting drunk, counted out the months since I'd last stood face to face with people I loved and realized I wouldn't see them in person any time soon. And right when it felt like it might become too much to bear, Verzuz announced its 10th "battle": Erykah Badu vs. Jill Scott." (McFarland, para. 1)

McFarland is fatigued, like many others, as the pandemic continued longer than expected. She emphasizes the frustration she carried as she watched people ignore CDC restrictions, choosing to congregate when many—who were obeying the CDC's recommendations—were suffering from lack of physical touch, quality time, and discontinuing their daily routines. The mental angst somewhat alleviates when "The First Ladies of Vezuz" was announced on May 1, 2020. That moment yielded hopefulness, anticipation and expectation as Black women sat on the edge of their seats awaiting the day—and Scott and Badu did not disappoint.

Defining the event as a "battle" would be incorrect. Scott and Badu, both from Generation X, contributed heartily to the Neo-Soul genre in the early 1990s. From the moment the two approached the screen, they began to smile and to complement each other. They took the time to reminisce when they first met at the House of Blues in Los Angeles. A shaven head Badu watched

Jill Scott perform on stage. After Badu played "You Got Me," which Scott originally wrote, they discussed each other's impact on the other upon first meeting:

Badu: You sang with such passion and such intention—I couldn't help but cry. You didn't see me out there, but I was right there.
Scott: But I saw you when you came backstage, and I didn't know what to do, and I regretted that. I was overwhelmed when I saw you. At the time, I was just in awe. It was that kind of night.

Rumors said that Scott and Badu had a "silent rivalry" in 1999 as Badu rose to fame after her 1997 debut Baduizm. Scott was a spoken word artist in North Philadelphia, her hometown, and had connected with Questlove of the Roots, who invited her to sing for their fourth album, *Things Fall Apart*. However, The Roots label, MCA Records, heard the song and forced for Badu to replace Scott's track—even at the protest of Badu, who still says Scott's version is the better one—to "recoup costs, along with achieving a mainstream hit" (Turner-Williams, 2020, para. 3). The hit led to Badu's third Grammy win for Best Rap Performance in 2000. To reconcile the damage the label had caused, The Roots invited Jill Scott on a tour where she was recorded live singing "You Got Me," which ended up on the *Roots Come Alive* album in November 1999. In July 2000, Scott released her debut album, the critically acclaimed Who Is Jill Scott?: Words and Sounds Vol. 1. The album gave Scott her first Grammy nomination as an artist for Best R&B Album in 2001. Badu's homage to Scott during the Verzuz battle revealed the sisterhood that Scott and Badu had for each other, and that which Black women maintain in a society that often pit Black women against each other.

As the two singers continued throughout the night, Black women on Twitter reacted with deep satisfaction and appreciation for the moment, which occurred when, like McFarland, many were longing for a reprieve from the weight of the pandemic. It was as if someone smudged sage throughout the house and rid of all the demons. Activist and MSNC correspondent, Brittnay Packnett, tweeted, "We all agree that Jill & Erykah was not a battle, but it was a shea butter balm, and we were the real winners, right" (Packnett, 2020)? Former First Lady Michelle Obama commented, Thanks for sharing some much-needed love (Obama, 2020). Twitter user, JessRossTheBoss, articulates the ethos of the night:

Black people are truly the heart, & soul of this world. Y'all hear this? Y'all feel this? We are in the middle of a worldwide pandemic and Erykah Badu and Jill Scott are giving us these hours of pure peace. A blessing. #Verzuz (Jess, 2020)

Thus, the competitive nature of battles before, all featuring male artists, producers, and songwriters, had then disseminated when Scott and Badu stepped into the ring. The "battle" transformed into a necessary Sunday Service at a Black church with a bombastic choir that moves the parishioners from pain to praise to prostration. After their healing circle, their streaming numbers tripled to 217 percent on all music-streaming platforms, according to Verzuz and Billboard. Their history of producing and releasing incensed lyrics flanked in herbal tea, headscarves and fusing of jazz, hip-hop, and soul contributes to their large viewership. They communicate, produce, and offer a sense of healing during a global pandemic when many are isolated from their friends, families, and communities. Ono and Sloop define vernacular discourse as "culture: the music, art, criticism, dance and architecture of local communities" (1995, p. 20). Vernacular discourse engages oppressed communities and the language they use to navigate historical and social events. Verzuz is a prime space for that.

Patti LaBelle vs. Gladys Knight.

Like Scott and Badu, Gladys Knight and Patti LaBelle's virtual event also brought a sense of sisterhood and storytelling. Meeting as girlfriends who have seen, heard and "done it all," they stood as elders—reaping the harvest of their labor and counseling the youth. Both born in 1944 (Baby Boomers), their vernacular is comprehended across generations of Black women. They have lived through Jim Crow, segregation in the North and South, the Civil Rights Movement and Sex Revolution. They have sung for presidents and sold-out concert venues across the world. In an industry that has dismissed and degraded many Black women artists, they have stood the test of time, and they are iconic to the Black community.

In *The Signifying Monkey: A Theory of African-American Literary Criticism*, Henry Louis Gates (2014) calls it "a blackness of the tongue" (p. xix). Black people, especially Black women, have developed a coded language that is exclusive, private, and personal. With music older than Scott, Badu, Brandy, and Monica, the two soulful legends have the highest viewed show of all Verzuz events, doubling their music streaming on Apple Music and Spotify (Gunn, 2020). Their coming together represented more than sisterhood, but the history and foundation that current Black female artists (and other races) have built their entire careers trying to emulate, model and achieve. Moreover, it was the night that Black women—elders and younger—shared.

It would be disrespectful to call the Verzuz event between LaBelle and Knight a battle. They both came to prominence in the 1970s with other Black female soloists, including Diana Ross, Aretha Franklin, and Shirley Caesar.

The singers collaborated with Dionne Warwick on their Grammy-nominated songs "Superwoman" and "That's What Friends Are For." Both LaBelle and Knight had warmed their way into the hearts of younger generations, including guest appearances on television, including "A Different World" when LaBelle played Dwayne Wade's mother, and Knight made a guest appearance performing "Love Overboard" with characters Whitley Gilbert (Jasmine Guy) and Jaleesa Vinson (Dawnn Lewis).

From Patti hitting her knee as she tried to famously kick off her shoes and Gladys having to stand up to hit the high notes, saying, "I can't make that note sing down," the event was what Hunter Harris of Vulture names, "It wasn't anthem against anthem or hit against hit: This was a reunion" (Harris, 2020). A family reunion among Black people is an enclave public where Black Americans meet in a centralized location with immediate and distant relatives and descendants of the family's patriarch and matriarch. In their coming together, there is a hearty helping of food (usually barbecue or "soul food" known as comfort food), games like spades and activities for children. A Black family reunion is exclusive to that local community, and that community shares a vernacular and discussion that other communities cannot participate, but to only witness.

For the first thirty minutes, Knight and LaBelle caught up on life, grandkids, and recipe secrets that they refused to share with anyone outside of each other. Using words like "child," "honey," "baby," and "Bebe Kids," they spent as much time as they wanted to delve into issues from the upcoming election, people who they both knew and loved who have died (Luther Vandross aka and pronounced Lutha), and crime. "Gladys, we been through," says Patti. "Been through" is a common phrase used among older Black people to signify hardship or troubles. One would often hear in a church or a community setting, "I'm going through," from someone who is having a challenging time financially, relationally, or emotionally.

Moreover, the "been" denotes that they have overcome it. Black women can relate to the "been through" of the early months of the pandemic and Black people's brutalization by police like Breonna Taylor. Interestingly, there is no need to explain what the "through" usually is, but understood that it is debilitating, hard and heavy to bear.

LaBelle: Girl, we talk the same talk.
Knight: We sure do.

The rhetoric of "talking the same talk," implies that they have shared experiences within the music industry, some that they cannot share with the enclave of Black women fans during a livestreamed event. It is like another common saying in the Black community, "I see what you puttin' down," and even a more contemporary saying among millennial women on social media, "I see you, sis." The implication here is Black women, generationally, empathize well with other Black women. They share similar experiences, feel similar pains from romances, faith, and social positioning of Black women, and they are willing to stand together and support one another.

"Auntichella" quickly became the name dubbed this event. The name "auntie" is often given to Black women in the Black community who are sisters of parents, full of love, kindness, and closeness to their sibling's kids. It has since evolved into an epithet given to older Black women in film, media, and politics who present as warm, bold, and robust in what she says and unafraid to whom she says them. Gladys and Patti have embraced the role of matriarchs in the music industry, admittingly requiring a level of respect from all persons.

As they went down a list of younger singers they loved, Patti referred to the younger singes as "little heifers," a term of endearment that is not meant to be offensive but confirming a bodacious talent. It was Knight who took the chance to openly rebuke Monica and Brandy who had engaged in a Verzuz a month before. Knight yelled toward the screen, "Yall, work it out!"

In her southern dialect, reminiscent of a grandmother, aunt or older woman, called for the fighting between two Black youths to an end, "make up" and "go play nice" at those family reunions. Their demand for Brandy and Monica to "work it out," was a call to sisterhood as well as professionalism (and many fans requested a tour together). Besides, Monica and Brandy only possessed one Grammy between them—the one they both won for "The Boy Is Mine." While the other female-led events were resplendent of comradery and ease, the ethos of Monica and Brandy's *battle* was a watershed moment.

Monica vs. Brandy.

R&B powerhouses and songbirds, Monica and Brandy, ushered the most anticipated event of the franchise. The two had not sat down eight years, both in their early 1940s. The beef between Brandy Norwood and Monica Brown is quite unclear. While they both acknowledged during the Verzuz event that they were unsure where or how the contention started, they admitted that the music industry played a hand in making them compete against one another. In 1997, Brandy and Monica released "The Boy Is Mine," earning them their first and only Grammy. According to Atlanta producer Dallas Austin, Monica "hit" Brandy backstage at the MTV's Video Music Awards in 1998 before their performance of "The Boy Is Mine." Monica, who was sixteen and has since apologized, blamed the incident on being immature and had since apologized. The incident is something that Monica has often tried to dissipate as she maneuvered through her career.

Monica admitted to struggling with public perception during the early years. She was only twelve-years-old when she recorded "Like This and Like That" and "Before You Walk Out My Life." The latter, written by Andrea Martin, was initially for Toni Braxton's Secrets album. Monica's developed voice, mature lyrics and southern dialect contributed to the world seeing her as older, sassy, and short-tempered in her youth. Monica's adultification' contributes to the erasure of Black girls' innocence (Epstein et al., 2017). Research shows that adults are more likely to view Black girls between the ages of five and fourteen as adults than white girls. Identifying a Black girl as "sassy" or "grown" often leads to their experiences of being punished at higher rates than white girls. Black girls classified as "hood" or "ghettoing her" are defined as not easy to work with, loud, and angry, attaching them to the Angry Black Woman stereotype.

On the other hand, Brandy had hits such as "Sittin' Up in My Room" at age fourteen, which has lyrics considered more age-appropriate for a teenaged girl. As Brandy continued to grow in her career and christened as "The Vocal Bible," she received mentorship from icons including Whitney Houston. Compared to Monica's Atlanta upbringing, Brandy was raised mostly in California after her family moved from Mississippi. The early years of her career afforded her opportunities such as playing Cinderella in Roger and Hammerstein's *Cinderella,* acting roles alongside legends like Diana Ross in *Double Platinum* and staring in a tv-sitcom, *Moesha,* for six seasons. However, Brandy's girl-next-door persona diminished in the early 2000s. In 2002, twenty-three-year-old Brandy appeared on the Oprah Winfrey Show and announced she was married and pregnant. However, Brandy revealed in a 2014 interview with Winfrey that she lied in 2002 (Capretto, 2017). While she was indeed pregnant with her first child, she was not married. She admitted to feeling "the pressure of having to be perfect."

In Sister Citizen: Shame, Stereotypes and Black Women in America, Melissa Harris-Perry argues that Black women often approach political, cultural, and institutional structures as if they are walking into a crooked room. The crooked room demands Black Women make themselves upright (2011, p. 29) when it is the room that is bending, off-kilter and corrupt. These spaces often criminalize Black women for not aligning themselves to accommodate everyone else, and when they do, they suffer even more. Harris-Perry expounds on how shame affects Black women. Black women feel shame they "transgress a social boundary or break a community expectation" (2011, p. 106). When Black women have performed outside of social expectations, such as having children unmarried, they feel shame, "our bodies react with hormones that tell us to save our social selves by fleeing." Brandy fled from the spotlight to prepare for motherhood. However, she also fled to avoid criticism and shame.

Monica and Brandy confronted the same monsters at different fulcrums of their lives: combating stereotypes that labeled them as too grown, too fast, and not being perfect enough. Collectively, they spoke to the enclave of Black women who fought to ignore, avoid, and deconstruct systems that pigeonholed women to unrealistic and hegemonic standards of sexuality and femininity. From their hits such as "Don't Take It Personal" to "Almost Doesn't Count," Monica and Brandy spoke to and for a generation of women who were learning to define themselves for themselves.

Before the runs and the riffs commenced, Monica and Brandy started the event by offering condolences to Chadwick Boseman's family, the Black Panther actor. He died on August 28, 2020. They later acknowledged Vanessa Bryant, Kobe Bryant's wife, who was killed in a helicopter accident in January 2020 alongside his daughter, Gianna.

Monica: The level of devastation we all have experienced in the last year is unprecedented.
Brandy: It's unbelievable
Monica: We could not have foreseen it. And I thank God for his grace and mercy, and I pray I don't offend anyone that we both feel that way. To everyone suffering so much, we pray we can bring a little bit of joy through our music and the arts.

This emphasis on faith, religion, and spirituality is another shared experience of the Black woman vernacular. A 2014 Pew Research analysis showed that Black women are more religious than Black men, white men, and white women. (Cox & Diamant, 2020) According to the report, 80 percent of Black women said religion is important to them, 79 percent pray daily, and 89 percent are devout in their belief in God. When one attends a local church or religious institution and organization, it is common to find more women in the pews than men. Black women depend on a higher source and form of spirituality to overcome or sustain the political, social, and systemic oppression experienced by Black women. From the weight of the pandemic to the summer uprisings against injustice, Monica and Brandy imply that their rich and hearty catalogs of chart-topping R&B provide joy and solace for the evening. Before the night's event, the fans prepared for that joy. Sylvia OBell, a media personality, tweeted, "We are in dire need for the joy that will be Brandy and Monica's #Verzuz tonight" (O'Bell, 2020).

When candidate Kamala Harris appeared on a screen behind the women before the battle—appealing to voters—the stars responded, "We got you," implying using their platforms of influence to corral voters to the polls, especially in Georgia, where Stacey Abrams led voter mobilization efforts. Alongside providing good music, Black women across entertainment and political spectrums worked together to push Democrats over the finish line on November 4, 2020.

Eyes were particularly concerned about their beef, which they addressed before the battle. As Verzuz continued to grow, fans tweeted and started social media posts about whom they would want to see in potential battles. Monica and Brandy were highly requested. Monica addressed that producer Missy Elliot begged her to join Brandy in a Verzuz, which Brandy agreed to do before Monica conceded to the partnership.

Brandy: She's probably the only reason you're here. Thank you, Missy.
Monica: Don't do that, friend. I really wanted to come because I wanted to speak to you face to face. I feel like the more we're talked about, the more it led for it to be difficult, unnecessarily. I'm a straight shooter, and I really admire what you've had to endure musically and personally. I don't know all of it. You're the real deal.
Brandy: Absolutely, and I just need you to know that I have the utmost love and respect for you, no matter the times where it seemed like I didn't. For someone to start at 12 years old, the longevity of your career. You never gave up no matter what you've been through, and you're still here. Period.

Addressing another Black woman with "friend" is a common epithet used my millennial and Gen Z Black women, sparked by Black women social media personalities such as PrettyGirlVee and B. Simone. It's a term of endearment like "sis," "baby," and "boo" also used commonly among younger generations of Black women. Also, "period" is used as a declarative form of expression used by generations of Black women. Rap duo, City Girls, have popularized the term, asserting the speaker's confidence and validity in their preceding statement.

Monica's desire to approach Brandy after eight years, in person and public, is what most Black women echo as "coming to you as a woman." It means that if there is an issue that requires resolution, two women resolve it together rather than allowing that issue to fester, magnify or circulate on social media, gossip blogs or pop culture media outlets. Monica's appeal is one of admiration for Brandy, an understanding that both endured more behind the scenes and cameras than fans would ever know. Brandy returns the compassion, acknowledging that endurance and commending Monica for her successful career. Here, they both divorce themselves from the negative stereotypes associated with them from previous years. They both have children now and are still making music that reaches the ears of thousands of fans. They both commit to "put away childish things." Even within the few awkward moments and cringy personality quirks of both, the reunion of lifelong friends, sisters, and colleagues was the real winner of the night. Black women empathize with "squashing" beef, especially one formed from misunderstandings and early years of immaturity. The coming together of Black women, whether one is #TeamMonica or #TeamBrandy, is how communities are established, sustained, and protected in perilous times.

CONCLUSION

In conclusion, this chapter highlights how female-led Verzuz events were the most successful livestreamed franchise events due to the collective vernacular Black women share, especially during political and social unrest in America. It is vital to recognize that what connects Black women with other Black women is storytelling of pain and love, trials and triumphs in a world that significantly oppresses them and their experiences. Black women evolved Verzuz from a battle viewed from a hand-held device to a meeting space for Black women, comparable to churches, family reunions, and girls' night out. Black women created space during the global pandemic to recognize, acknowledge, and comfort other Black women. This chapter is a starting point for further theoretical, methodological, and empirical data, reflection, and narratives about Black women. Verzuz's ability to coalesce generations of Black women into one digital, networked space is admirable and contributes to its success. Hopefully, this work will amplify how Black women's common vernacular not only saves Black lives but builds communal, digital spaces where Black women are humanized and protected.

REFERENCES

A Tribe Called Jess, [@JessRossTheBoss]. (2020, May 9). *Black People are Truly the Heart & Soul of This World. Y'all Hear This? Y'all Feel This?* [Tweet]. Twitter.

Artiga, S., Corallo, B., Pham, O., & Orgera, K. (2020, June 3). Growing data underscore that communities of color are being harder hit by COVID-19. *KFF.* https ://www.kff.org/policy-watch/growing-data-underscore-communities-color-harder -hit-covid-19/.

Capretto, L. (2017, December 7). The big lie brandy told Oprah—And why she did it. *HuffPost.* https://www.huffpost.com/entry/brandy-oprah-lie-married_n_5635331 ?guccounter=1&guce_referrer=aHR0cHM6Ly93d3cuZ29vZ2xlLmNvbS8&guce_ referrer_sig=AQAAANsQZMTiBBb2YNt0vErqipKo4ZtK-hdvP2FHOfpNImx 1s12TDSm7l0Nn5UuiELsVhiK8dko-WLeCDOUlTYirUaWquyM6o1j-i588qmh 4Rlt7SR3GgRLLNUf66GdWcO70kQ7rZxR071DXhQd4DO_EGUoxSykoTN 0E0oHJHyf-LuRk.

Cochrane, N. (2020, August 11). The Verzuz effect. *Billboard.* https://www.billboard .com/articles/news/cover-story/9430242/verzuz-effect-swizz-beatz-timbaland-inst agram.

Cox, K., & Diamant, J. (2020, September 10). Black men less religious than black women, but more religious than white women, men. *Pew Research Center*. https://www.pewresearch.org/fact-tank/2018/09/26/black-men-are-less-religious-than-black-women-but-more-religious-than-white-women-and-men/.

Epstein, R., Blake, J., & González, T. (2017, July 18). Girlhood interrupted: The erasure of black girls' childhood. *SSRN*. https://papers.ssrn.com/sol3/papers.cfm?abstract_id=3000695.

Florini, S. (2019). *Beyond Hashtags: Racial Politics and Black Digital Networks*. New York University Press.

Gates, H. L. (2014). *The Signifying Monkey: theory of Afro-American Literary Criticism*. Oxford University Press.

Gunn, T. (2020, September 22). Patti LaBelle and Gladys Knight broke personal streaming records after Verzuz battle. https://www.revolt.tv/news/2020/9/22/21451546/gladys-knight-patti-labelle-streaming-verzuz.

Harris, H. (2020, September 14). The Patti LaBelle–Gladys Knight Verzuz was a gift. *Vulture*. https://www.vulture.com/2020/09/review-patti-labelle-gladys-knight-verzuz.html.

Harris-Perry, M. V. (2014). *Sister Citizen Shame, Stereotypes, and Black Women in America*. Yale University Press.

Hobson, J. (2008). Everybody's protest Song: Music as social protest in the performances of Marian Anderson and Billie Holiday. *Signs: Journal of Women in Culture and Society*, 33(2), 443–448. https://doi.org/10.1086/521057.

Neal, M. A. (2020, November 30). Patti LaBelle, the Doyenne of Philadelphia soul. *The New York Times*. https://www.nytimes.com/2020/11/30/t-magazine/patti-labelle-philadelphia-soul.html.

Obama, M. [@michelleobama]. (2020, May 9). *Thanks for Sharing so Much Needed Love* [Tweet]. Twitter.

Obell, S. [@sylviaobell]. (2020, August 31). *We are in Dire Need for the Joy that will be Brandy and Monica's #Verzuz Tonight*. [Tweet]. Twitter.

Ono, K. A., & Sloop, J. M. (1995). The critique of vernacular discourse. *Communication Monographs*, 62(1), 19–46. https://doi.org/10.1080/03637759509376346.

Packnett, B. [@mspackyetti]. (2020, May 9). *We All Agree That Jill & Erykah was Not a Battle, But It was a Shea Butter Balm, and We Were the Real Winners, Right?* [Tweet]. Twitter.

Person. (2020, November 27). Verzuz battles brought us together to bond over live music again. *Salon*. https://www.salon.com/2020/11/26/verzuz-battles-brought-us-together-to-bond-over-live-music-again/.

Reynolds, K. (2016, July 5). Lemonade, black femininity, and vulnerability. *Hooligan Mag*. http://www.hooliganmagazine.com/blog/2016/4/28/lemonade-black-femininity-and-vulnerability.

Stamberg, S. (2014, April 9). Denied a stage, she sang for a nation. *NPR*. https://www.npr.org/2014/04/09/298760473/denied-a-stage-she-sang-for-a-nation.

Turner-Williams, J. (2021, January 9). The story of the roots' "you got me": Why Jill Scott's version reigns supreme. *Okayplayer*. https://www.okayplayer.com/music/jill-scott-erykah-badu-verzuz-you-got-me.html.

Waddell, R. (2016, October 14). Beyonce's formation tour sold over 2 million tickets and made over $250 million. *Billboard*. https://www.billboard.com/articles/business/7541993/beyonce-formation-tour-2-million-tickets-250-million-dollars.

Williams, K. (2016, July 1). Beyoncé brought her formation world tour to wales and it was amazing. *WalesOnline*. https://www.walesonline.co.uk/whats-on/music-nightlife-news/beyonc-brought-formation-world-tour-11551204

Williams, V. (2020, April 8). U.S. government is urged to release race, ethnicity data on covid-19 cases. *The Washington Post*. https://www.washingtonpost.com/politics/government-urged-to-release-race-ethnicity-data-on-covid-19-cases/2020/04/06/7891aba0-7827-11ea-b6ff-597f170df8f8_story.html.

Chapter 5

DJ's Gig

Affective Hip-Hop Culture and Affordances of Participatory Platforms during a Global Pandemic

June Mia

During the first week of a government-mandated shutdown as a result of the COVID-19 global pandemic, a Hip-Hop DJ named Derrick Jones (aka D-Nice) threw an epic party through the platform Instagram Live (IG Live) dubbed #ClubQuarantine or CQ. Unlike any other event before it, the party consisted of D-Nice livestreaming his DJ set on IG Live with over 100,000 users. The mass audience that tuned in to Derrick Jones' performance on Instagram Live experienced an affective ambiance that shifted the way DJs use platforms for their work. Instagram has become a conduit for affective expression (Papacharissi, 2015) of Black culture, reflexively experienced through participation. Participation is a significant part of Hip-Hop culture, heavily relying on people coming together and utilizing public spaces where community members can communicate unrestricted by old obstacles (Kitwana, 2005, p. 78). D-Nice utilized his IG Live account as a perceived affordance (Davis, 2020), an opportunity offered to a perceiver (Clarke, 2003). D-Nice created an opportunity and facilitated an experience many people will not forget. When much of the United States was under mandatory stay-at-home orders, the 1980s Hip-Hop artist created another lane for the culture—the Insta-club scene. In conjunction with the pandemic, this event also generated a response from other DJs to adapt the way they perform on participatory platforms. Using preliminary data from an ongoing online survey of Hip-Hop DJs, my research examines Hip-Hop DJs' participation with social media and how the pandemic changed how they promote their work online.

Shortly after the Center for Disease Control (CDC) declared a pandemic on March 11, 2020, D-Nice began to perform on IG Live. The global pandemic prevented people from attending traditional social gatherings, and it eliminated many gigs for DJs. In an interview with the Breakfast Club (Breakfast Club Power 105.1 FM, 2020), D-Nice said #ClubQuarantine arose from loneliness and frustration. His gigs were canceled, and there was a moment of grievance. He then describes a calmness coming over him to "be still." He opened up his IG Live and began to play music rather than DJ. At first, a small number of people stopped in to talk and be present with one another. By day three of going "live" on Instagram, he "felt different" because of the number of people participating. When there were 2,000 people on his IG Live, he began to DJ, and there was an immediate spike of users watching him perform including musical celebrities (e.g., Drake). In 2020, Americans collectively experienced several unprecedented events; fortunately, we also experienced this particular occasion. In his virtual interview with Breakfast Club DJs—Angela, DJ Envy, and Charlamagne Tha God—he expressed his joy. "I'm glad that it came from a person from our community, you know, like just a Hip Hop person in general, to bring the world together . . . in a virtual party which is just beautiful to experience."

Hip-Hop has always been inventive and collaborative, and Black DJs have a rich history of technological innovation within American culture (Fauch, 2006). Bell hooks (1992) discusses how Blackness is vital because it invites engagement in a revolutionary ethos that dares to challenge and disrupt the status quo. D-Nice's IG Live party is revolutionary for music and culture. Although D-Nice describes #ClubQuarantine as a real party, a place for solace, and a community where people connected, it was also a strategic move by this 1980s DJ. He knew he was onto something significant and important with his IG Live performance. During #ClubQuarantine, IG Live users came together in an ephemeral place to hear music from the past mixed in with the present. People were experiencing something together; this included celebrities from film, music, and politics. D-Nice engaged with people by calling out their names as he saw them comment or join the viewers on IG Live. As he played his set, he was also working the room. He explains in his Breakfast Club interview how celebrities' PR representatives would call him and give him a heads up about their "arrival." The comments and discussions also fueled his drive for more participation. He saw a comment about everyone being there except for the Obama's. He spent time calling around in an attempt to get former First Lady Michelle Obama into his IG Live, and it happened. For over a decade, Internet researchers have called for a departure from thinking about the Internet as a separate place from reality. This event (CQ) is an important opportunity to reconsider academia's approach to researching the Internet. Society and culture are identified and experienced *through* the Internet instead of merely *on* the Internet.

Online participatory platforms afford users the ability to communicate and create together, building a network that can prove beneficial to both artist and consumer and the industry and culture as a whole. Participatory online platforms' dynamic infrastructures affect how cultural production unfolds (Duffy, Poell, & Nieborg, 2019). Henry Jenkins first coined the term "participatory culture" in 1992 to describe the cultural production and social interactions of fan communities. He defines the phenomenon of participatory culture as one that "is emerging as the culture absorbs and responds to the explosion of new media technologies that make it possible for average consumers to archive, annotate, appropriate, and recirculate media content in powerful new ways" (Jenkins, Purushotma, Weigel, Clinton, & Robison, 2006, p. 8). In addition to Jenkins et al., other researchers have considered the relations between the development of participatory culture and the evolution of new media technologies, and the expansion of communities invested in media production and circulation (Barney, Coleman, Ross, Sterne, & Tembeck, 2016). Jenkins and Deuze's discussion of how technology has converged (2008) demonstrates how the DJ has become a cultural signifier based on *what* and *how* music is played, revealing significant insight about the culture and the audience.

Participatory online platforms (e.g., Instagram, Twitch) have substantially increased the collaborative process by allowing participants to blur the line between production and consumption. DJs can now communicate with fans in new ways (beyond the traditional limits of convention meet and greets or random sightings). The affordances of two-way communication have created new forms of labor for people who participate in online spaces. Labor is the "exertion of the body or mind . . . usually used to describe activities that have some compulsion attached to them" (Hesmondhalgh, 2010, p. 276). Ongoing research about emotional labor (Hochschild, 1979; Senft, 2008), relational labor (Baym, 2015), and visible labor (Abidin, 2016) of digital citizens and their engagement on participatory online platforms demonstrates the complexity for users and the labor they experience online. As a platform, Instagram provides a space for different models and modes of communication (e.g., linear models (Shannon & Weaver, 1949) and two-way models). Instagram's unique affordances have also created new ways of communicating that not all online platforms offer (such as real-time engagement through livestreaming). Instagram introduced IG Live in November 2016 in response to Snapchat and Periscope (owned by Twitter). Livestreaming is the live broadcast of the actor's activities (Johnson & Woodcock, 2019). Twitch emerged as an early two-way online platform with a specific audience for people playing video or computer games (Johnson & Woodcock, 2019);

more recently, because of D-Nice, there has been an influx of Hip-Hop DJs livestreaming their performances on Twitch. This intimate interaction with the audience increases DJs' labor, especially relational labor (Baym, 2015).

As media evolve, so do the roles of a Hip-Hop DJ and, to understand what is happening in culture, researchers can utilize tools, frameworks, theories, and analysis methods. As our media landscape continues to adapt to and alter the capabilities of the Internet, media companies continue to shift and change society's entertainment access. From my ongoing research project, I share how DJs have reimagined affordances. DJs have become more active on platforms that allow performance to supplement or even become their primary income source. In the case of D-Nice, his weekend of playing music on IG Live for hours at a time resulted in a significant sponsorship from Ford Motor Company (2021, Ford Media Center). Moreover, several companies approached him with additional sponsorship opportunities, which he turned down because they did not align with his brand.

This alignment of one's brand with other companies is a strategy used among many microcelebrities. Senft (2013) describes microcelebrity as an approach to online behavior, constituted by "the commitment to deploying and maintaining one's online identity as if it were a branded good, with the expectation that others do the same (p. 346)." Technology and Hip-Hop have developed a symbiotic relationship that affords an economy of artistry and labor ecology. DJs can transition into microcelebrity status on platforms like Instagram, mainly because they utilize promotion and relational labor platforms. In their research about German musicians and their labor economy, Mühlbach and Arora (2020) found through interviews that the music industry is more focused on promoting the artist-brand rather than the music; as such, the musicians are encouraged to sell themselves in hopes of opening up other streams of revenue.

Instagram's original community manager stated in an interview that there are specific behaviors that Instagram users practice when hoping to achieve influence, including (1) leveraging existing social networks, (2) using hashtags, and (3) connecting with the larger Instagram and digital photography community (Marwick, 2015, p. 147). These are all practices that D-Nice employed during the virality of #ClubQuarantine. The term *virality* is a metaphor, ironically for what we are experiencing in a pandemic, referencing how quickly a contagious virus spreads from one host to another (Khan & Vong, 2014). This term is often used with electronic-word of mouth marketing (e-WOM), especially with the way online users share content and information as networks. This chapter explores how the events of #ClubQuarantine enlightened other DJs to the real affordances (Davis, 2020) of platforms for gigs when they are no longer able to perform in traditional spaces like clubs and outdoor festivals. In the following sections, concepts like the gig economy, participation, and relational labor are more fully explained before analysis of results from a survey assessing the affordances of participatory platforms for Hip-Hop DJs during the pandemic, and concluding with limitations and discussion.

GIG ECONOMY

The Internet is an advertising-based medium (McChesney, 2013) and the act of "performing self" can be commodified. Research on identity expression on Twitter shows various performative approaches that resemble being famous, being a brand, and being a commodity (Marwick & boyd, 2010; Papacharissi, 2011). The architecture of an online participatory site is what allows the promotion of the user as a brand. With the emergence of Web 2.0, the online universe now consists of interactive environments that enable multiple interaction formats—"not just site-to-user, but user-to-user and user-to-public" (Walter et al., 201, p.34). Interactive environments and platforms have changed how people work and the number of people considered as gig workers. A *gig* is a slang term for work introduced into the American dialect in 1950 through jazz by way of Black culture (Baym, 2018). A *gig* is a short-term employment that tends to be unstable (Baym, 2018). According to the Bureau of Labor Statistics (2017), 55 million people in the United States are gig workers. This number accounts for approximately 34 percent of the U.S. workforce and was projected to increase to 43 percent in 2020 (International Labour Organization, 2019). The *gig economy* concept helps establish a capital-labor relationship between an actor and a digital participatory platform that mediates workers' supply and the consumer's demand to complete a small task (i.e., gig) (Friedman, 2014). Gandini's research on the gig economy suggests understanding the platform as a digital-based point of production, intended as the place where the labor process is enacted upon workers (Gandini, 2019, p. 1040). For DJs, their labor entails playing music for the crowd, being a library for music, and knowing when to play the song. They build momentum and set the mood—bringing to the foreground listeners' memories and at times evoking or creating nostalgia because music is woven into the cultural fabric. Among many other forms of labor, the DJ's labor includes online interactions such as Q&A with fans on IG Live, a Facebook live performance, and the recording of a video shared on YouTube.

New opportunities emerge and continue to evolve in the communication media fields. Although tech companies like to think of themselves as "just" platforms, researchers like Hesmondhalgh (2017) argue that tech companies incorrectly deny their role as media outlets. This denial allows these corporations to disregard specific regulatory structures enforced by the Federal Trade

Commission (FTC), which protects consumers and enforces antitrust laws, and the Federal Communication Commission (FCC), which regulates communications. Recently, Instagram announced plans for monetization, emulating other platforms like Twitch, which already incorporates many ways for users to be paid by their subscribers. On April 24, 2020, Facebook announced it was launching Messenger Room, which will host up to fifty people at one time (with no time limit), along with various other changes to allow for its users to connect more easily ("Introducing Messenger Rooms," 2020). Their Facebook webpage also mentions their interest in augmented reality and virtual reality—which shows the agility and cross-medium flexibility of Facebook. Just four days later, Facebook announced it would add a payment method during livestreams for entertainers. We have seen a shift in American cultural production due to the social, institutional, and economic penetration of specific media platforms (Nieborg & Poell, 2018), resulting in platformization. Nieborg and Poell define *platformization* as "the need for cultural producers to be visible for platform-specific contexts, or how 'producers . . . are impelled to develop publishing strategies that align with the business models of a platform" (Nieborg & Poell, 2018, p. 8). D-Nice demonstrates platformization within and around his Instagram page. Platformization, defined by Helmond (2015, p. 1) and rooted in software studies, is "the extension of social media platforms into the rest of the web and their drive to make external web data platform ready." According to Nieborg and Poell (2018), platformization marks the reorganization of cultural production and circulation, rendering cultural commodities contingent (p. 4290). DJs have learned to monetize their art because music sits along a spectrum—between art and business, artistry and commodity. As DJs become increasingly recognizable by the public and build extensive fanbases, they become more influential due to their ability to capture their audiences' attention and affection.

As the days of #ClubQuarantine progressed, D-Nice's famous March 21st performance thrust him into the role of both DJ and cultural signifier among other identities, but he is not the only DJ making a living from online performances. More recently, DJs began including in their Instagram profiles links to Venmo (digital wallet) and Cashapp (mobile banking). The DJ's ability to grow in recognition and power on a platform has gone from only recently possible to profitable. More and more, users are focusing on self-branding tactics. Self-branding occurs through social media. Microcelebrity serves as "a self-presentation technique in which people view themselves as a public persona to be consumed by others, use strategic intimacy to appeal to followers, and regard their audience as fans" (Marwick, 2015, p. 333). Gandini's research suggests that people recognize these platforms not only as places to interact socially but, moreover, as a digital-based point of production intended as the place where the labor process is ascribed upon workers

(Gandini, 2019, p. 1040). The gig economy turns workers with legislated employment rights into independent contractors who individually must fend for themselves (O'Donnell & Zion, 2019, p. 228).

#ClubQuarantine inspired other Hip-Hop DJs to increase their participation online and perform on IG Live—invitations to online sets and parties began to pop up in my Facebook newsfeed. There was chat about it on Twitter and posts on Instagram. My alma mater's DJ Josh Aguirre (DJ Beatstreet) decided to host an online "HUB Party," which resulted from a few Facebook conversations about D Nice's #ClubQuarantine." The "HUB" party is what we called an event usually put on by the university's Black Emphasis Committee, a group of students who created programs that emphasized Black culture. It was held in the Hadley Union Building (HUB) at Indiana University of Pennsylvania. Several alumni worked to promote the university-sponsored event on Instagram, Facebook, Twitch, and anywhere else people could be reached the first time DJ Beatstreet performed. The HUB party lasted for 2 hours and 45 minutes and had 253 viewers, with 215 actively engaged in the chat of the livestream. In conjunction with the HUB party, people gather on Zoom to experience the event together. Over seventy-five IUP alumni, spanning over a decade in graduation dates joined in on a private Zoom as they also listened to DJ Beatstreet perform online. Although these numbers are not as voluminous as D-Nice's #ClubQuarantine in terms of participants, it demonstrates the opportunities afforded to even those who are not considered celebrity DJs and is an example of how people engage in the culture through reimagined practices.

PARTICIPATING IN THE CULTURE

Hip-Hop allows people to look at American society from a perspective alternative to the dominant narrative about American culture—one that is aware of political, economic, sociotechnical, and cultural realities of people of color. American Anthropologist Clifford Geertz understood culture, not as a stage with actors and performance like Canadian Social Psychologist Goffman (1959), but as a system of symbols embedded in social action: "the culture of a people is an ensemble of texts, themselves ensembles (Geertz, 1973)." According to Barney et al. (2016), participation is when people are involved in doing something and taking part in others. It comprises a relational aspect—a part of society and culture. It is constructed with the concept that one can be actively involved with others in decision-making processes that affect the evolution of social bonds and communities' systems of knowledge in organizations, politics, and culture (Barney et al., 2016, p. viii). Those who participate in Hip-Hop tend to be more aware of the African Americans' experiences in America. Black feminist sociologist, Patricia Hill Collins, clarifies how racism has created a separate communal structure for African Americans where a culture of resistance exists apart from the dominant structure (Collins, 2000, p. 226; Steele, 2014, p.14). As our media landscape continues to adapt to and alter the Internet's capabilities, media companies will continue to shift and change society's entertainment access, which in turn, will alter how we participate, as seen recently with #ClubQuarantine. Platforms like Instagram are remediated from media before it. Remediation is when media diverges from and reproduces older media and adjusts to the new media's changes (Bolter & Grusin, 1999; Deuze, 2006). We can see how DJing on Instagram is a new form of performing at the block party or the club, as we did with D-Nice's #ClubQuarantine. Participatory online platforms' dynamic infrastructures affect how cultural production unfolds (Duffy, Poell, & Nieborg, 2019). Rogers calls for a departure from "the virtual/real divide" (2013, p. 33) and instead proposes an approach to Internet research that may ground its claims to understand society and culture identified *through* the Internet, as opposed to merely *on* the Internet.

Participatory platforms provide artists with the ability to express themselves—they can control and shape their image and online persona. Out of the top twenty most-followed Instagram accounts, nine are musicians (eight women and one man) (Boyd, 2020, February 21). It is not surprising that the male artist with the highest number of followers on Instagram is Justin Bieber – this is likely in part because he found his fame on YouTube and could be considered a digital native. Musicians use social networking sites to engage with their audience. On Instagram, Beyonce has 165 million followers, DJ Khaled has 23 million followers, and D-Nice now has 2.5 million. Musicians find themselves with an ability to "speak" directly to their fans through these platforms resulting in new forms of participation and labor.

In the 1970s, many Hip-Hop DJs were limited in resources yet found ways to reappropriate technology and emerging cultural forms of communication (Rose, 1994). Although communication media (like the Internet and social networking sites) afford people an amplified voice and encourage connectivity, people face experiences that are not so utopian. In 2002, a company conducted a survey about the Hip-Hop Generation and concluded that African American youth were "the most influential trendsetting youth market in the world" (Kitwana, 2005, p. 95). Influence is a tangible idea when we look at one particular example—the Tik Tok dance "Renegade," which grew in popularity and went "viral" in 2019. This dance, created by fourteen-year-old Jalaiah Harmon, became an Internet sensation; however, people did not initially credit Jalaiah as the inventor. Although Hip-Hop may have begun within the Latinx and Black community, there are numerous instances of cultural appropriation or "culture banditry," which is an appropriation that comes in the form of an outsider ripping off another culture (Kitwana, 2005, p. 124). There is also "acknowledged appropriation," whereby outsiders emulate a culture and refine it while acknowledging its roots (Kitwana, 2005, p. 124). Eventually, Jalaiah was recognized for her role in the dance's creation; however, the oversight of recognizing a young Black dancer's contribution in the dominant narrative is an example of the type of culture banditry that can occur online. Tricia Rose discusses how important it is to locate Hip-Hop culture within the context of America's history. Hip-Hop expressions like rap provide alternative views from a dominant narrative, dance also being an extension and expression of culture. Black cultural experience is often articulated and expressed through music, and Hip-Hop is a fundamental matrix of self-expression for generations (Rose, 1994). The significance of people showing up to #ClubQuarantine is as much a head nod to Black culture as it is to D-Nice's role within Hip-Hop. Over 100,000 users came together because of a Hip-Hop DJ's virtual performance. Users online can participate because of the environment and architecture of these platforms. The Internet presents several opportunities for people that can be understood as affordances.

Affordances

American Psychologist J. J. Gibson (1977) developed affordance theory. His work asked people to look at the environment used by an entity and the complementarity of the entity and the environment. Gibson describes how "an affordance points both ways, to the environment and the observer" (para. 11). Davis (2020) describes affordances as how objects shape an action for socially situated subjects (p.6). Hip-Hop DJs had a knack for perceiving affordances in certain technology when others did not. For example, DJ Kool Herc, a Hip-Hop pioneer, introduced the "merry-go-round" technique—the process of rotating between different records with comparable beats and breaks (Katz, 2012), and it was a precursor to modern-day DJing. In the case of D-Nice, we can look at how he utilized Instagram's architecture and environment to engage with other users, perhaps foreshadowing a future trajectory for DJs. Platforms afford users with different capacities of participation through functions such as display, discovery, search, and ultimately the consumption of a cultural artifact distributed through search engines and digital databases (Morris, 2020). For instance, Instagram as a platform has many affordances designed for a personal account (e.g., livestream, photo upload, direct message), and additional affordances for those who opt-in as a professional account (e.g., access to analytics). Once a user opts-in for a professional account, there are further distinctions between business and creator. J. J. Gibson (1977) describes how "the observer may or may not perceive or attend to the affordance, according to their needs, but the affordance, being invariant, is always there to be perceived."

D-Nice understood how IG Live could make an impact, even if he was not fully aware of the extent of this impact at the time. In using his intuition, he was able to produce a meaningful interaction for his audience. Instagram affords the DJ's audience the ability to express support through comments and emojis and now through direct payments. For many musicians who want to make money, participatory platforms can generate opportunities for two-way interactions between fans and the artists. One of Instagram's functions affords users to participate using hashtags. Hashtags—a function of many social networks—are integral to online participatory platforms as they "form, re-form, and coordinate information" (Bruns & Burgess, 2015) related to key terms. Hashtags provide a new way to form communities and power discourse based upon particular experiences (e.g., a particular tour, concert, album, or song). Access to the event and how people connect online can influence popularity quickly. The hashtag #ClubQuarantine' was used throughout the media resulting in significant advertising and subsequent increase in audience. In her work about musicians and the intimate work of connection, Nancy Baym (2012) states that musicians move in worlds where music is the basis of their friendships with one another, with other people in music, and with their audience members in different locations (p. 49). As musicians or celebrities move about the world, these hashtags can create a space for people to come together to discuss the same topic. D-Nice was able to garner thousands of new Instagram followers in response to his performances on IG Live; however, if it were not for specific affordances, perhaps this phenomenon would not have happened. The ability to perform anywhere with a cell phone and Instagram account affords a new type of engagement. Instagram afforded users the ability to share #ClubQuarantine not only with the use of the hashtag but also with sharing functions that further encouraged direct E-WOM. Although D-Nice created and curated a special experience with music, the audience also played a significant and critical role. CQ shows how livestreaming added value and fostered participation. Mühlbach and Arora's (2020) research found a shift in societal values and argued a potential for the devaluation of culture due to the streaming industry. The researchers discussed how digital artifacts, like the downloadable song or the streaming twenty-four-hour movie rental, have decreased the demand for cultural assets. However, these digital artifacts also make media consumption more agile and accessible, as we see with the DJ's performance.

Research using cyber ethnography demonstrates how users who engage with one another on Instagram have a stronger sense of familiarity with the other (Dupont, 2020, p. 657). "By making oneself accessible and helping fans develop a greater affinity with their work, musicians can develop a fanbase invested enough to spend money on them (Baym, 2011, p. 5)." Although people may have more access to these types of affordances, it does not mean that this #ClubQuarantine phenomenon can happen for anyone. D-Nice expended significant labor and time building his brand. His access to the masses was due, in part, to the work he put into building relationships with people long before the pandemic arose.

Relational Labor

Hip-Hop's identity is shaped and reshaped through meaning-making and experiences of communities and subcultures interacting with the genre. Social interactions and relational labor must be addressed when discussing the meaning-making of cultures (Philips & Hardy, 2002). In this age of instant connection, people place expectations on experiencing music together—this expectation is an acknowledgment or response—usually from artist to audience and audience to artist. This process combines production and consumption. The modern-day performing DJ can be seen not just as an artist but also as an intermediary who participates in a culture's meaning-making. Many types of labor go into participating in the community. One of the types of labor is relational. Nancy Baym (2015) defines relational labor as ongoing interactive, affective, material, and cognitive work of communicating with people over time to create structures that can support continued work (Baym 2015, p. 19). "Artists must balance their own, sometimes competing economic and social needs with their audiences' needs to connect with them and with one another" (Baym 2015, p. 14). Online users engage in relational work as they follow, like, comment upon, and share content. These interactions increase the user's value to companies or businesses looking to advertise back to the audience.

The "relational" aspect encompasses creating and maintaining connections with people sans payment, all while attempting to earn money outside of the relational labor. It is the go-between for professional work and personal relationships. On social media, relational labor can take the form of a response to a question, a call out in a livestream, or any behavior assessed by the receiver as a connection. At the same time, fans can exhibit this type of work by maintaining an online presence and conducting themselves as members of the culture: posting, commenting, sharing, and providing insight into their private lives. The musical experience can be an economical one, and, as Baym (2018) discusses in her book, *Playing to the Crowd*, the value of musicians' work has always been one of reciprocity. Baym (2018) researches musicians and their use of relational labor to foster their careers. She assesses how music can cultivate subcultures and how music can draw people together while simultaneously creating boundaries for where culture exists. D-Nice's sets on IG Live consisted of many forms of labor, including relational.

Affect

Baym (2018) states that the more technically mediated society becomes the more value is placed on public embodied performances of authentic natural feelings. These feelings may be interpreted as affect. Affect has often been described poetically in academia as something lying between the physical and the emotional, or "a semi- or preconscious bodily response in the meeting between the subject and the world surrounding the subject" (Dilling-Hansen, 2015; Massumi 2009; Thrift 2008). According to Papacharissi (2010), affect captures "the intensity of drive or movement with a not yet developed sense of direction" (p. 21). More research needs to be conducted on affect, as Andre Brock calls for studies of cultural online performance to incorporate both the intended and the unintended audience's technologically and culturally mediated reception of that performance (Brock, 2020). Whereas some researchers describe how "the affect framework shows how audiences can intensify affect in the theater and impact the felt quality of the performance" (Pais, 2016, p. 1). We can see affect online in behaviors surrounding Twitter uprisings using hashtags (Meraz & Papacharissi, 2013) and news being collaboratively collected (Papacharissi & Oliveira, 2012). It is also felt on the floors of Jamaica's dancehalls (Henriques, 2010) and between the performer and the audience (Pais, 2016). This affective ambiance can also help describe #ClubQuarantine. There was an affective response to a livestream with the DJ and the audience. For anyone who has been to a club or dance party, it is not difficult to understand how music affects the vibe of the room or how the lights interacting with the bass of a song create a feeling—this feeling can also be created in a livestream of your favorite DJ during a Friday night at #ClubCorona or #ClubEssential. A coexperience from participants in an IG Live or Twitch performance introduces an affective labor. "Who influences and who is influenced, are questions that can no longer receive a clear answer" is a quote Blackman and Venn (2010) use by Vincianne Despret (2004, p. 115) when discussing the relationship between mammals and the way they respond to one another. This is an appropriate metaphor to describe the DJ and the audience—whether mediated or in-person.

Audiences, Fans, and Fandom

According to Ang (2006), the audience is a collection of spectators, a group of individuals who gather together to attend a performance and "receive" a message "sent" by another (p. 27). Others take a more theatrical paradigm and recognize the audience as the premise of an event (Pais, 2016), whereas the audience re-affects the stage or the performer. Although audiences may have been composed of spectators in the past, they no longer consist of an unknown group or mass audience to the industry. This is due in part to datafication of consumers' online user behavior. Analytics provide insight to companies and users and help determine who these users are and even how they feel (through sentiment analysis) based upon certain behaviors (e.g., music requested on streaming platforms, engagement to posts).

There is also a certain subtype of audience member, one who may be considered a fan. Fans are "associated with the cultural tastes of subordinated formations of the people, particularly those disempowered by any combination of gender, age, class, and race" (Fiske, 1992, p. 30). To Henry Jenkins (2006), "online fan communities might be some of the most fully realized versions of Levy's *cosmopedia*, expansive self-organizing groups focused around the collective production, debate, and circulation of meanings, interpretations, and fantasies in response to various artifacts of contemporary popular culture (p. 137)." One aspect of fandom as derived through consideration of fashion and style, including fan purchases of artist merchandise through fan clubs. Baym (2015) argues that commercial markets can be integral to specific participatory communities because fans buy tickets, clothing, and other memorabilia. Artists on tour typically offer special fan gear available only for a limited time, creating a demand for consumers to participate in these events. With performances on participatory platforms, these unique fan products are now in the form of emoticons for those who purchase subscriptions to a user's channel for the month/s and year. There is also a push for merchandise to be sold on Instagram's most recent update of a shopping page called "Shop" that was previously just for photos. Instagram has expanded into a shopping platform, a concert venue, and a meme station since it launched in 2010 and was subsequently acquired by Facebook a few years later in 2012 (Macon, 2017).

Several scholars have researched and analyzed fandom (Booth, 2015; Jenkins, 2008; Lewis, 1992) and the parasociality of celebrities and fans online (Baym, 2012; Marwick & Boyd, 2011). A parasocial relationship is a celebrity-fan relationship in which the "ordinary" person knows much about the celebrity, but the celebrity knows nothing about the fan (Ouvrein, Pabian Machimbarrena, De Backer, & Vandebosch, 2018). Senft (2008) looks to sociologist Stanley Milgram's work about the social convention when explaining what she calls "strange familiarity." The expression is a response to sociologist Stanley Milgram who uses the term "familiar strangers" to refer to people who know each other by sight but not by name (such as people from the same yoga studio who attend class at the same time but do not speak with each other). The behavior is essentially an unspoken agreement not to engage with one another beyond a quick nod and a smile.

However, this relationship changes when one person spends time watching or commenting on the celebrity's images and posts shared on a platform like Instagram. According to Senft (2013), "these scenarios move us from being familiar strangers to individuals bound in strange familiarity: the familiarity that arises from exchanging private information with people from whom we are otherwise remote" (p. 352).

This parasocial behavior can enhance celebrity culture by providing fans with more opportunities (outside of traditional performances such as television shows, movies, and concerts) to engage with their favorite celebrity. More importantly, this alternative form of engaging with celebrities can provide fans with greater insight into the lives of these celebrities as they are often afforded more intimate details than would be otherwise known from watching a movie or listening to an album (e.g., seeing how a celebrity decorates their home or getting a chance to see them playing with their pet). These additional insights can allow a fan to see and a celebrity to share, their more "authentic self" (or in perhaps many situations, allows the celebrity to carefully cultivate a fake "authentic" self to share with fans—a potential negative ramification of participatory platforms).

Fandom includes the communication between those with similar interests. For instance, participation is a significant component of Hip-Hop. The "call-and-response" engrained in the Hip-Hop genre is a part of the history of orality in African American culture. African American oral culture is demonstrated in physical spaces like barber and beauty shops, nightclubs, and in mediated environments (Steele, 2014, p. 8) like blogs and social networking sites. Online fan communities are where users can develop relationships with others of similar fan interests (Baym, 2010). As these communities form, they tend to share their knowledge because no single fan can know everything necessary to appreciate the content fully (Jenkins, 2006). Some describe fandom as a conveyor for, and means of, self-discovery, affirmation, and friendship that moves from object to object as identities and circumstances change across a lifestyle (Baym, 2015). Similarly, fandom is a collective strategy by communities of people who evade dominant ideologies set forth by the corporations who try and set the discourse. There are times where the fans will also "call out" a celebrity for inauthenticity, like a bad photoshop edit on Instagram.

Haynes and Marshall's (2018) work argues optimistically for the way new media offer participatory experiences for those interacting within the entertainment industry—including the music industry. The monetization of social media has afforded musicians the ability to make money from their audience. Studies show how social media users can become influential and persuasive to those who have similar identities and likes as their followers or have favorable aesthetics. DJs are positioned to have meaningful connections with people because music is a connective and influential source. The research on Hip-Hop DJs' impact on society is valuable when we look at how many people identify with the genre. In a survey by YouGov (Nguyen, 2018), they found that half of the country believes Hip-Hop and rap best represent America.

METHOD

In this next section, I discuss the questions used to guide my implementation of a survey to assess how DJs experienced shifts in their participation online during a global pandemic. When analyzing culture, some argue a researcher must read and interpret, rather than utilize quantitative methods that model natural sciences inquiry (e.g., hypotheses, observations, measurements, conclusions) (Cook, Clayton, Herbert, & Middleton, 2003). Kitwana (2005) suggests that Hip-Hop is nearly impossible to research quantitatively (p. 91), arguing instead that one must analyze Hip-Hop discursively (textually); however, I believe it is essential to integrate both quantitative and qualitative analyses to obtain a robust understanding of the industry. To understand the DJ's gig and affective labor within Black culture, we must explore how DJs utilize participatory platforms to engage with their audience and engage with the culture. Thus, the general questions driving the survey are the following:

 RQ 1) How do DJs use participatory platforms for performance and self-presentation?
 RQ 2) What forms of labor do DJs engage in on these platforms during the pandemic?
 RQ 3) How have DJs reimaged the affordances of these platforms due to the pandemic?

These questions help us think about the affordances of platforms for the gig worker (i.e., a club DJ, a Hip-Hop DJ), and how culture is sustained for people when we are encouraged to stay home rather than interact in public spaces. As we understand how people significant to a culture adjust to global issues like a pandemic, we may also understand how events like #ClubQuarantine sustain Black music and how important participation is to the sustenance.

Data Collection

The data collection program utilized was Qualtrics, a software that allows for questionnaires to be collected, captured, stored, and analyzed. Stata, a general-purpose statistical software program was used to run further statistical analysis. The survey is a self-administered online data collection that was distributed through different forms of social networking sites: Instagram, Facebook, and Twitter. The data collected is a nonprobability sampling conducted through snowball sampling of users who identify as a DJ, and it is an ongoing data collection on DJs. The specific question, "Do you consider yourself a DJ?" was a qualifying question for the questionnaire. This survey resulted in fifty respondents; upon removing respondents who did not meet specific criteria, this ongoing survey resulted in twenty-eight qualifying participants.

These respondents answered questions about group identity as DJs and the types of platforms they use to connect with other DJs, their online audience, and people outside of online platforms. I also account for DJs who make their own mixes and stream their own performances online, as D-Nice did on IG Live. Several statistical analyses were conducted on the data points across different DJs, demographic characteristics, use of platforms, and social media use during the pandemic depending on race, and age. Tabulations were run to determine descriptive statistics. The types of DJs who took part in the survey consisted of people who consider themselves either a club, radio, wedding, or tour DJ, performer DJ, or some mixture of the aforementioned.

FINDINGS

Prior to the pandemic, 95.65 percent of my respondents performed in-person. When asked how much the pandemic has changed the way the DJ performs, 92.31 percent said the pandemic changed the way they performed from some degree to completely. Of the respondents, 60 percent stated they used a new platform since March 2020 when Disaster Proclamations were being issued (specifically in Chicago). These platforms consisted of Facebook for livestreaming, MixCloud, Twitch, IG Live, Web radio, Zoom, and Restream which is a cloud multistreaming service. A total of 89 percent of the respondents create their own mixes and 75 percent of them livestream. Almost all DJs who took this survey used online platforms and 96 percent used Instagram as a platform to engage with community.

The DJs who responded to the survey ranged between the ages of eighteen and over fifty-five, with the average age in the twenty-six to thirty range ($SD = 0.3$). More than half of the respondents identified as male (68%), whereas females made up 28 percent and those who identified as other 4 percent. The mean earnings were between $10,000–$19,999 ($SD = 0.34$). A total of 85 percent of the respondents spent time outside of what you consider work to practice their skills on a weekly basis.

Limitations

The sample as a whole is small ($n = 28$); however, the findings are insightful because of the unique population and situation (performing during a pandemic). Unfortunately, the sample size does not accurately account for the representation of race and gender. Respondents who identified as Black was 14 percent of the sample population, whereas 85 percent was non-Black. Another limitation is that not all DJs who took this survey are exclusive to Hip-Hop, but play genres that include techno, pop, and Latinx. Therefore, the results may not be generalizable to other populations.

DISCUSSION

Based on this preliminary analysis, it is clear that DJs are savvy gig workers who utilize the tools afforded to them. Although some of these platforms are not used by DJs to engage with their audience (81% did not use Tik Tok), DJs are active on Instagram. Respondents primarily used Instagram to promote themselves as a DJ and felt group identity within their role through use of the platform. Research shows that community and culture can be captivated online. During the pandemic, DJs were able to find new ways of performing whether it was from a new streaming site or social media platform.

The type of labor the DJs engage in has expanded further online. During COVID-19, they continued to be a cultural signifier while reimagining what culture can look like during a pandemic. This includes encouraging people to subscribe to their channels, or responding to questions. The labor includes setting up profiles to different platforms, making mixes, uploading them, and sharing online. This labor DJs experience includes practice because DJing is a skill.

The reimagining of these platforms seems to be at the discretion of affordances from each platform. I asked questions about several platforms, just to get names of platforms I hadn't thought of or heard about. There can be an infinity of platforms, but it is not the platform that holds the most importance. This is because we can experience society and culture *through* the Internet instead of merely *on* platforms. To analyze communities or the ambiance of platforms, we must look at the features of the platforms and how communities form around them, as well as the themes of self-presentation that emerge from digital artifacts. A survey can capture certain kinds of data points, but qualitative methods can provide much deeper knowledge. A tool called Critical Technocultural Discourse Analysis ("CTDA") can be used to investigate phenomena on a participatory platform where a researcher can analyze the discursive behavior of users, corporations, and platform (Brock, 2018). CTDA is used to interrogate technology as cultural representations and social structures. In forthcoming research, I plan to use quantitative and qualitative methods to study the phenomena of DJing during a pandemic in conjunction with the traditional nonpandemic experience. The DJ story provides insight into not only labor and affordances but also how culture can be sustained through participation. Hip-Hop DJs are artists and innovators, serving as intermediaries who collaborate with their audiences in cultural meaning-making. Since its inception in the mid-1970s, Hip-Hop has been a collaborative process. Black and Latinx youth invented Hip-Hop in the South Bronx, and it has transcended from an art form into ideology (Chang, 2006; Rose, 1996). The construction of meaning in Hip-Hop occurs reflexively through communities' participation and experiences. Participatory platforms like Instagram remediate the space where DJs perform.

In this chapter, I discussed several theories (i.e., gig economy, affordances, relational labor, and participatory platforms) and applied them to the experience of D-Nice's #ClubQuarantine. The survey results on DJs' social media use during the COVID-19 pandemic provide insight into a shifting digital landscape. This work is significant because it captures a historical event and provides insight as to how people alter and increase their participation through online platforms during times when in-person performances are limited or altogether prohibited.

REFERENCES

Abidin, C. (2016). Visibility labour: Engaging with influencers' fashion brands and# OOTD advertorial campaigns on Instagram. *Media International Australia, 161*(1), 86–100.

Ang, I. (2006). *Desperately Seeking the Audience*. Routledge.

Aires, S. (2020). Laboured identity: An analysis of user branding practices on Instagram. *tripleC: Communication, Capitalism & Critique. Open Access Journal for a Global Sustainable Information Society, 18*(1), 494–507.

Barney, D., Coleman, G., Ross, C., Sterne, J., & Tembeck, T. (Eds.). (2016). *The Participatory Condition in the Digital Age* (Vol. 51). University of Minnesota Press.

Baym, N. K. (2010). Rethinking the music industry. *Popular Communication*, Special issue on the recession, *8*(3), 177–180.

Baym, N. K. (2011). Social networks 2.0. *The Handbook of Internet Studies, 2*, 384.

Baym, N. K. (2012). Fans or friends?: Seeing social media audiences as musicians do. *Participations, 9*(2), 286–316.

Baym, N. K. (2015a). *Personal Connections in the Digital Age*. John Wiley & Sons.

Baym, N. K. (2015b). Connect with your audience! The relational labor of connection. *The Communication Review, 18*(1), 14–22.

Baym, N. K. (2018). *Playing to the Crowd: Musicians, Audiences, and the Intimate Work of Connection* (Vol. 14). NYU Press.
Blackman, L., & Venn, C. (2010). Affect. *Body & Society, 16*(1), 7–28.
Booth, P. (2015). *Playing Fans: Negotiating Fandom and Media in the Digital Age.* University of Iowa Press.
Boyd, J. (2020, February 21). The top 20 most followed accounts on Instagram. Retrieved from https://www.brandwatch.com/blog/top-most-instagram-followers / on April 27, 2020.
Breakfast Club Power 105.1 FM (2020, June 19). D-Nice talks club quarantine impact, mental health + the healing power of music [Video file]. *Youtube.com.* Retrieved from https://www.youtube.com/watch?v=LMbibLzNYrc
Brock, A. (2018). Critical technocultural discourse analysis. *New Media & Society, 20*(3), 1012–1030.
Brock Jr, A. (2020). *Distributed Blackness: African American Cybercultures* (Vol. 9). NYU Press.
Bruns, A., & Burgess, J. (2015). Twitter hashtags from ad hoc to calculated publics. In N. Rambukkana (Eds.), *Hashtag publics the power and politics of discursive networks* (pp. 13–28). Peter Lang.
Chang, J. (Ed.). (2006). *Total Chaos: The Art and Aesthetics of Hip-Hop.* Civitas Books.
Clarke, E. F. (2003). Music and psychology. In Cook, N., Clayton, M., Herbert, T., & Middleton, R. (Eds.), *The Cultural Study of Music: A Critical Introduction* (pp. 113–123). Routledge.
Collins, P. H. (2000). *Black Feminist Thought: Knowledge, Consciousness, and the Politics of Empowerment.* New York: Routledge.
Davis, J. L. (2020). *How Artifacts Afford: The Power and Politics of Everyday Things.* MIT Press.
Despret, V. (2004). The body we care for: Figures of anthropo-zoo-genesis. *Body & Society, 10*(2–3):111–134.
Dilling-Hansen, L. (2015). Affective fan experiences of Lady Gaga. *Transformative Works and Cultures, 20.*
Duffy, B. E., Poell, T., & Nieborg, D. B. (2019). Platform practices in the cultural industries: Creativity, labor, and citizenship. *Social Media + Society, 5*(4), 2056305119879672.
Dupont, T. (2020). Authentic subcultural identities and social media: American skateboarders and Instagram. *Deviant Behavior, 41*(5), 649–664.
Final FTC Agreement Represents a New Level of Accountability for Privacy. (2020, April 24). Retrieved from https://about.fb.com/news/2020/04/final-ftc-agreement/
Ford Media Center (2021, January 11). Ford launches 2021 F-150 with new lifestyle campaign featuring 'club quarantine' DJ D-nice. *Ford Media Center.* Retrieved from https://media.ford.com/content/fordmedia/fna/us/en/news/2021/01/11/ford-2021-f-150-club-quarantine-dj-d-nice.html
Fouch, R. (2006). Say it loud, I'm black and I'm proud: African Americans, American artifactual culture, and black vernacular technological creativity. *American Quarterly, 58*(3), 639–661.

Friedman, G. (2014). Workers without employers: Shadow corporations and the rise of the gig economy. *Review of Keynesian Economics*, 2(2), 171–188.

Gandini, A. (2019). Labour process theory and the gig economy. *Human Relations*, 72(6), 1039–1056.

Geertz, Clifford. 1973. Thick description: Toward an interpretive theory of culture. In Geertz (Ed.), *The Interpretation of Cultures* (pp. 3–30). New York: Basic Books.

Gibson, J. J. (1977). The theory of affordances. *Hilldale, USA*, 1(2), 67–82.

Goffman, E. (1956). The presentation of self in everyday life. Edinburgh: University of Edinburgh. *Social Sciences Research Centre*, 5.

Haynes, J., & Marshall, L. (2018). Beats and tweets: Social media in the careers of independent musicians. *New Media & Society*, 20(5), 1973–1993.

Helmond, A. (2015). The platformization of the web: Making web data platform ready. *Social Media + Society*, 1(2), 205630511560308. https://doi.org/10.1177/2056305115603080

Henriques, J. (2010). The vibrations of affect and their propagation on a night out on Kingston's dancehall scene. *Body & Society*, 16(1), 57–89.

Hesmondhalgh, D. (2010). User-generated content, free labour and the cultural industries. *Ephemera: Theory & Politics in Organization*, 10(3/4), 267–284.

Hesmondhalgh, D. (2017). Capitalism and the media: Moral economy, well-being and capabilities. *Media, Culture & Society*, 39(2), 202–218.

Hochschild, A. R. (1979). Emotion work, feeling rules, and social structure. *American Journal of Sociology*, 85(3), 551–575.

Hogan, B. (2010). The presentation of self in the age of social media: Distinguishing performances and exhibitions online. *Bulletin of Science, Technology & Society*, 30(6), 377–386.

hooks, b. (1992). *Race and Representation*. Boston: South End Press.

International Labour Organization (2019). Helping the gig economy work better for gig workers. Retrieved from https://www.ilo.org/washington/WCMS_642303/lang--en/index.htm

Jenkins, H. (1992). *Textual Poachers: Television Fans and Participatory Culture*. Routledge.

Jenkins, H. (2006). *Fans, Bloggers, and Gamers: Exploring Participatory Culture*. New York University Press.

Jenkins, H., & Deuze, M. (2008). *Convergence Culture*. New York University Press.

Jenkins, H., Purushotma, R., Clinton, K., Weigel, M., & Robison, A. (2006). *Confronting the Challenges of Participatory Culture: Media Education for the 21st Century*. Chicago, IL: The MacArthur Foundation.

Johnson, M. R., & Woodcock, J. (2019). "And Today's Top Donator is": How live streamers on Twitch. tv monetize and gamify their broadcasts. *Social Media+ Society*, 5(4), 2056305119881694.

Katz, M. (2012). *Groove Music: The Art and Culture of the Hip-Hop DJ*. Oxford University Press on Demand.

Khan, G. F., & Vong, S. (2014). Virality over YouTube: An Empirical Analysis. *Internet Research*.

Kim, J. H., & Yu, J. (2019). Platformizing webtoons: The impact on creative and digital labor in South Korea. *Social Media+ Society*, 5(4), 2056305119880174.

Kitwana, B. (2005). *Why White Kids Love Hip-Hop: Wankstas, Wiggers, Wannabes, and the New Reality of Race in America*. Civitas Books.

Lewis, L. A. (Ed.). (1992). *The Adoring Audience: Fan Culture and Popular Media*. Psychology Press.

Macon, J. (2017). User-generated content: An examination of users and the commodification of Instagram posts. *Available at SSRN 2944502*.

Marwick, A., & boyd, d. (2011). To see and be seen: Celebrity practice on Twitter. *Convergence, 17*(2), 139–158. doi:10.1177/1354856510394539

Marshall, L. (2015). 'Let's keep music special. F—Spotify': On-demand streaming and the controversy over artist royalties. *Creative Industries Journal, 8*(2), 177–189.

Marshall, P. D., & Redmond, S. (Eds.). (2016). *A Companion to Celebrity*. Hoboken, NJ: Wiley Blackwell.

Morris, J. W. (2020). Music platforms and the optimization of culture. *Social Media+ Society, 6*(3), 2056305120940690.

Marwick, A. (2015). You may know me from YouTube: (Micro)-celebrity in social media. In Marshall, P. D. & Redmond, S. (Eds.), *A Companion to Celebrity* (pp. 333–350). John Wiley & Sons Inc.

McChesney, R. W. (2013). *Digital Disconnect: How Capitalism Is Turning the Internet against Democracy*. The New Press.

Mühlbach, S., & Arora, P. (2020). Behind the music: How labor changed for musicians through the subscription economy. *First Monday*.

Nagy, N. (2015). Imagined affordance: Reconstructing a keyword for communication theory. *Social Media + Society, 1*(2), 205630511560338. https://doi.org/10.1177/2056305115603385

Nguyen, H. (2018). Americans believe that rap and hip-hop best represent today's America. *YouGov*. Retrieved from https://today.yougov.com/topics/entertainment/articles-reports/2018/05/22/one-two-believe-rap-and-hip-hop-best-represent-tod

Nieborg, D. B., Duffy, B. E., & Poell, T. (2020). Studying platforms and cultural production: Methods, institutions, and practices. *Social Media+ Society, 6*(3), 2056305120943273.

O'Donnell, P., & Zion, L. (2019). Precarity in media work. In Mark Deuze and Mirjam Prenger (Eds.), *Making Media: Production, Practices, and Professions* (pp. 223–234). Amsterdam University Press.

Olson, C. A. (January 11, 2021). Instagram's plan to help music artists monetize the platform. *Forbes*. Retrieved from https://www.forbes.com/sites/cathyolson/2021/01/11/instagrams-plan-to-help-music-artists-monetize-the-platform/?sh=73809fe573f0

Ouvrein, G., Pabian, S., Machimbarrena, J. M., De Backer, C. J., & Vandebosch, H. (2018). Online celebrity bashing: Wrecking ball or good for you? adolescent girls' attitudes toward the media and public bashing of Miley Cyrus and Selena Gomez. *Communication Research Reports, 35*(3), 261–271.

Pais, A. (2016). Re-affecting the stage: Affective resonance as the function of the audience. *Humanities, 5*(3), 79.

Papacharissi, Z. (2011). A networked self. In *A Networked Self: Identity, Community, and Culture on Social Network Sites*, 304–318. Routledge.

Papacharissi, Z. (2015). *Affective Publics: Sentiment, Technology, and Politics.* Oxford University Press.

Papacharissi, Z., & de Fatima Oliveira, M. (2012). Affective news and networked publics: The rhythms of news storytelling on# Egypt. *Journal of Communication, 62*(2), 266–282.

Pearson, R. (2010). Fandom in the digital era. *Popular Communication, 8*(1), 84–95.

Prey, R. (2016). Musica analytica: The datafication of listening. In *Networked Music Cultures* (pp. 31–48). London: Palgrave Macmillan.

Rogers, R. (2013). *Digital Methods.* Cambridge, MA: MIT Press.

Rose, T. (1994). *Black Noise: Rap Music and Black Culture in Contemporary America.* Wesleyan.

Seawood, L. W. (2016, April 11). What Instagram discovered in our first nielsen music study. Retrieved from https://medium.com/cuepoint/what-instagram-discovered-in-our-first-nielsen-music-study-de1a2740c005

Senft, T. M. (2008). *Camgirls: Celebrity and Community in the Age of Social Networks* (Vol. 4). Peter Lang.

Senft, T. M. (2013). Microcelebrity and the branded self. In A. Bruns, J. Burgess, & J. Hartley (Eds.), *A companion to new media dynamics* (pp. 346–354). Blackwell Publishing Ltd. 10.1002/9781118321607.

Shannon, C. E., & Weaver, W. (1949). *The Mathematical Theory of Communication.* Urbana: University of Illinois Press, 117 pp.

Smith, S. (2016). *Hip-Hop Turntablism, Creativity and Collaboration.* Routledge.

Steele, C. (2014). *Digital Barbershops: The Politics of African American Oral Culture in Online Blogs* (Doctoral dissertation). University of Illinois at Chicago.

Titlow, J. P. (2017, November 21). How Instagram became the music industry's secret weapon. Retrieved from https://www.fastcompany.com/40472034/how-instagram-became-the-music-industrys-most-powerful-weapon on April 27, 2020.

Thrift, N. (2008). *Non-Representational Theory: Space, Politics, Affect.* Routledge.

Walther, J. B., Carr, C. T., Choi, S. S. W., DeAndrea, D. C., Kim, J., Tong, S. T., & Van Der Heide, B. (2010). Interaction of interpersonal, peer, and media influence sources online. In Zizi Papacharissi (Ed.), *A Networked Self: Identity, Community, and Culture on Social Network Sites*, Vol. 17 (pp. 17–38). Routledge.

Chapter 6

Old Hits Verzuz New Technology

How a Pandemic Ushered Legacy Artists into Monetizing the Clout Economy

Jabari Evans

INTRODUCTION AND BACKGROUND

> Because it's a legacy, you can make money from it for a long time. But it's just—when you look at streams and the percentage that goes from publishing or the percentage of money from the little tiny fraction of money that you get as an artist. However, (Verzuz is) raising the valuation on the catalogs of Black legacy artists, especially producers and songwriters, in a way that will allow them to use social media to package themselves and possibly sell their publishing rights the way that a startup might sell to Google or Microsoft.—Mark M.*, YouTube Artist Relations Executive. (Personal Communication, December 10, 2020)

Even before COVID-19, it would've been an understatement to say that there has been a major shift in the last fifteen years in the music industry. The corporate powers of production (major labels) are no longer the primary distribution channel for musicians to find an audience. In particular, social media platforms that allow for livestreaming figure centrally as sites through which emerging creatives can do the networking, acquiring, and displaying the markers of status necessary to make them celebrities or entrepreneurs worthy of investment (Marwick, 2013). In regards to the music industry, social media, streaming services, and e-commerce platforms have also drastically changed the labor practices of established musical artists as they too now must move between and within platforms to self-promote themselves, professionalize, and sustain their careers. For instance, the work of both Baym (2018) and Watkins (2019) argues that social media has strengthened the intimate connection of fan communities by providing launching pads for these recording artists to speak directly to fans of their music, build personal relationships with them, and let them share in their creative process. With the COVID-19 pandemic taking away the opportunity for major artists to do live shows and in-person paid appearances, established celebrities also must rely far more on livestreaming to perform their catalog, maintain ongoing affiliations and connections with their fans online, rather than seem uncaring or unavailable.

These significant shifts toward live events and the creative process being broadcasted/livestreamed via social media and other digital tools for communication have likely been the most critical thing to building or maintaining a career as a contemporary cultural producer. The impact of COVID-19 on in-person immersive experiences makes it now all but impossible to practice celebrity with aloof distance. For all musicians, emerging and well established, the COVID-19 pandemic has drastically affected their ability to get spotlight from an audience. Where once they were allowed to be aloof and inaccessible in between shows, now they are relegated to being ever-present on social media or curating socially distanced live shows to even try to keep the attention of their fans. As a result of time in lockdown and social distancing, spaces of music production (rehearsal spaces, studios) and consumption (venues, nightclubs) have found themselves suddenly without purpose.

Given that context, this chapter focuses on the livestreaming event Verzuz, the webcast concert series created by Hip-Hop music producers Timbaland and Swizz Beatz. Conceived during the COVID-19 pandemic as a virtual DJ battle, Verzuz was originally conceived as a duel between unsung Hip-Hop music producers over Instagram Live broadcasts. The event has since grown to being a full professional production that is less a duel between Hip-Hop/R&B producers but now a virtual celebration of two legendary artists within Black music. Though still available on Instagram, the event is now live broadcast feed presented by Apple Music, is recorded using professional television studio equipment, teleprompters, and a simple character generator editing used to display viewer comments from Twitter. As of April 2021, Verzuz will be acquired as a part of the Triller Network. Triller is an American videomaking and social networking service owned by Proxima Media.

During my study of Verzuz, I have utilized practices grounded in ethnographic methods like conducting interviews, transcribing, and coding them. Given the limitations of in-person ethnography during the current COVID-19 pandemic, I employed digital urban ethnography (e.g., Lane, 2018) which privileges interpersonal communication with subjects via in-person as well as digital communication tools. Interview participants and social media subcultural groups were selected through a combination of purposive sampling from my own social networks, referrals from those in my social media network, and participant observation in the digital and physical social worlds of Verzuz performers and their audiences. All participants quoted in this chapter are anonymized unless having given written consent to be mentioned by name in my research. All names with a * indicate the usage of a pseudonym. This presentation draws on preliminary data analysis (coded using Nvivo) from digital participant observation and interviews collected in late 2019 as well as in-progress (and COVID-19 adjusted) data collection in 2020.

Ultimately, I will highlight the ways in which COVID-19 has disrupted the spatial practice of music. From there, I will argue that there is a need for new representational spaces of music, and that Verzuz offers a new form of musical-spatial practice, appropriating spaces of the domestic and the everyday, and fusing/overlaying them with new cultural meaning and what Taylor, Raine, and Hamilton (2020) term the "reconsideration of value" by potential consumers. Thus, the overarching objective of this chapter is to explore patterns of music streaming and social media usage surrounding Verzuz as a virtual live concert. More specifically, I ask what the material effects of Verzuz's large-scale webcasted live performances actually are on online audience activity, and also theorize how these performances can drive a new model of music monetization.

In doing so, I also explore Verzuz as an example of the ways in which virtual concerts can trigger artist exposure, revenue, and record listening in a moment when audience members cannot attend in-person music concerts but are far more engaged with social media for collective listening and are hyper-accessing the recordings of whichever artists they want via streaming services. In addressing the long-term impact of these new circumstances, I will conclude by suggesting the Verzuz battles have ushered "analog era" celebrities into a new arena of monetization and visibility for their talent. To conclude, I argue the ways in which Verzuz artists are accumulating digital clout demands new thinking and a new focus on the ways in which all musicians will now be forced to monetize their brands through digital practices and streaming platforms in more supplementary ways.

LIVE MUSIC IN THE MIDST OF A PANDEMIC

> The music industry is really struggling right now. I think that's because now that touring is off, the table people are realizing that a lot of the digital economy around music right now, if you look at it isolated from touring, it's not that sustainable for a lot of artists. It feels like they're just churning out a lot of content for free as a marketing stepping stone to drive sales of tours. Or sales of merch. Rather than having digital be really a core stand-alone experience. I think people took the touring cycle for granted. And now we're in a very extreme situation where in most areas of the world live shows don't exist. And so how do you

close that cycle in an interesting and sustainable way? Once you release an album can you make an online digital only experience that fans will pay for or that can at least close that gap in value that's been lost?

Those were the words of Cherie Hu (Aguilar, 2020a), an award-winning journalist, researcher and entrepreneur who has been covering the music business very closely for over five years. Like many, she spent the majority of 2020 working from home due to the COVID-19 pandemic, pondering what the future holds for artists in the industry she has dedicated her livelihood to. As someone whose job it is to think about monetization and new technological trends shaping the future of the music industry, she (like many industry insiders I spoke to) initially was almost certain that streaming would be the way that major labels would be able to escape the economic crisis of COVID-19. Even so, she was equally concerned that social lockdown would disrupt spatial practice of live music, fan appeal, and the financial livelihood of the recording artists. Echoing those same sentiments, prominent national Entertainment journalist Jerry L Barrow explained:

> I liked it at first. Now it's over. Not over, but it's not the same. It's like I don't know if you remember there used to be this thing called Jazzmobile used to have Grant's Tomb back in the day and folks would just roll up to Harlem during the summer. And I don't think anybody was listening to the music. It was just to go hang out and be seen. And after a while it just got to be so overwhelmed with people that it stopped being enjoyable. That's what social media has done to live music sets from DJs and other famous musicians. (Aguilar, 2020b)

Entertainment lawyer and artist manager Josh Kaplan elaborated on that point by speaking to the temporality of fan attraction to the live show presented digitally:

> Kids are going to go to shows. That's not going to die out. I think the whole surge to do these virtual shows—it's tough to make an impact now. When covid first started people were rushing to do that and it was cool. And for the first few months I didn't mind watching an artist perform in her bedroom or see some cool stuff. But I think that's going to go away to a certain degree. (Personal Communication, December 12, 2020)

Prior to the COVID-19 pandemic, the economy for live music and the record industry have both evolved and prospered extensively over the 2000s, with a particular growth being seen in the spawning of numerous music festivals (Naveed et al., 2017; Robinson, 2015) and various online music services (Holt, 2010; Wikstrom, 2013). Live music is still the best and primary source of income for artists, even in the midst of ubiquitous recorded music. Kjus and Danielsen (2014, 2019) argue that one reason for this may be that live music is perceived as a unique and rare musical experience—something that fans expect to be particularly intense and surprising, or, in short, to stand out from our everyday listening (Brown & Knox, 2017; Kjus & Danielsen, 2014, 2019). In her book on relational labor of musicians, Nancy Baym (2018) suggested that digital tools and technologies have only increased levels of fandom and enhanced the demand for in-person experiences with our favorite artists. Even so, the relationship between these musical domains (the live and the recorded) changed immediately due to COVID-19, with many negative ramifications for artists, concert venues, and audiences alike. Due to mandated social distancing, COVID-19 also presents a new set of challenges for those established artists who are seeing paid gigs to perform live dwindle and are struggling for impactful opportunities online to get intimate connections with their fans and supporters.

To be fair, prior to COVID-19, artists at the major artist level typically only used YouTube as depositories for their music videos. They might have only posted new videos six, seven times a year, if they released any music that year. Now, artists are being forced to act as if they are bloggers to stay relevant—chasing views and subscribers in the attention economy by posting every single day. As an artist manager and industry veteran from Los Angeles told me:

> Artists have to post every day now. Or at least once or a couple times a week. That's definitely a cadence that artists are not used to. And if you compare touring with that mechanic, touring is essentially playing the same show over and over again in different cities. And you could change the set list from one show to the next, but it's mostly the same, especially if you're building the tour around a specific album. Whereas once you're online and you can instantly reach a global audience, you have to constantly keep the content fresh. Otherwise people won't keep coming back. And that's definitely a skill and a mindset, an effort that a lot of artists didn't really feel the need to invest a lot of time in. Because That just wasn't' their forte. Their forte was making albums and then performing them in person. (Personal Communication, December 12, 2020)

According to my respondents, most of the musicians who were struggling to make this transition into the social media age pre-pandemic were either what one manager called "legacy artists" (those who had been in the business since the 1980s or before and had established audiences prior to the rise of social media) and "OGs." OGs were established artists throughout the shift from interacting with audience members primarily at shows and through mass media to also encountering them directly through social media. Additionally, there is a third category ("Blog-era" artists) of established musicians who got their start after or around Myspace began in 2002. Those people have never been musicians in a time when engaging fans through social media was not relevant to the job.

While the disruptions faced by musicians during COVID-19 pandemic clearly have significant economic implications for those concerned, they can also be seen as a crisis of spatial practice—one which poses larger challenges to musical practice itself. For many genres, the live music experience lies at the heart of practices of production and consumption, with livestreaming considered by some to "diminish the art." This valuing of the "live" experience further compounds the unwillingness of many musicians to utilize livestreaming as a stopgap during an economic crisis. Despite this, it would appear that fans and musicians have continued to offer support to one another via online communication, which suggests a willingness (at least for the time being) for established artists to continue to engage in practices that use livestreaming platforms as representational spaces for live music experiences and intimate connection.

VERZUZ: THE MEDIATED BLACK MUSIC FESTIVAL

What's going to happen if there are no shows and no one streams. What is the industry? A career foundation as an artist. It seems like a lost cause to me. And I think now a lot of people in music are realizing that what brought the recorded music industry back to a state of growth was the very lean back functional aggregation, like modeled for music. And I think now because people are stuck at home and actually crave more human connection, they're actually more open to engaging with artists on more direct to consumer channels as you would call it. So audio streaming in the aggregate has gone down, which is also very surprising to me. In contrast, maybe this is because the supply has gone up, but so many people are watching music live streams now. They're garnering hundreds and thousands and millions of views. Especially with these (live streaming) festivals.—*Cherie Hu*

As pointed out above by Cherie's quote from the Think Like a Rapper podcast (Aguilar, 2020), music and media are now deeply intermingled in the domain of live music. Various online resources and activities such as festival forums, music streaming of festival artists and festival-related content in social media have become the immediate surroundings of a festival—the contemporary mediated festival, that is, stretches far beyond its physical and temporal limitations (the here and now of the actual concert and the festival venue) into a virtual realm. According to David Hesmondhalgh (2013), live music events have grown from being mainly a co-present form of social publicness to mainly being mediated forms of social publicness via social networking platforms. Contrary to pre-COVID-19 times when there was a clearer line between co-present and mediated aspects (for example, live TV broadcasts), the virtual events held in a time of social distancing are buoyed by new forms of media and subject to a heightened level of mediated online publicness, creating a new form of live event that has both co-present and mediated aspects.

Related to this perspective, contemporary concert experiences (held with limited in-person capacity and broadcasted via livestreaming) are reliant upon "the new connectivity" of the audience (Wikstrom, 2009, p. 6). This connectivity is largely facilitated by social media, which allows for direct real-time communication during the event, and for, the "personalization of an otherwise anonymous group" (Baym, 2013, p. 224). In relation to the live music event, this means that in today's society, the audience has no choice but to encompass fans that are not physically present at the event.

Generally, the interplay between live music events and the media platforms surrounding them seems to have fresh momentum with the new Internet-based media and associated increase in participatory culture (Jenkins, 2006). This increase is premised on several factors, including the vast amount of information on the Internet, the availability of such information and the new conditions for simultaneity between the festival event, media activity, and access to recorded music. Events have gained greater significance in the media landscape thanks to these enhanced opportunities for real-time communication in online media, providing a framework for action through which emotional as well as mental affiliations can be constituted (Kjus & Danielson, 2019). In other words, in the twenty-first century, in-person events seem to provide a framework for action in the media landscape, working as attractors for attention and communication on social media and music-streaming platforms. Events may, for example, provide a structure or filter in terms of listening choice made from the "long tail" of music available in music-streaming services (Anderson, 2006; Maaso, 2016).

To be a social media "influencer" is often not associated with Blackness in modern understandings of mainstream fame and microcelebrity in digital spaces (see Duffy & Hund, 2015). This is true despite that Black culture has developed many members of today's digital vanguard and provided major innovative contributions to larger contemporary digital culture (Brock, 2020; Florini, 2020). That said, Black digital practice has become very much a mainstream phenomenon, even if its expert practitioners rarely receive proper recognition for their inventions, economic compensation for their participation (Brock, 2020). These issues are central to emerging conversations on why the innovations on visibility labor by Black musicians in digital spaces has largely been ignored in scholarly literature (Evans, 2020; Stuart, 2020). Black social media users often perceive and use these platforms in unintended ways, often changing the business direction of the platforms themselves (Florini, 2020). These innovations have allowed Black recording artists to amplify their involvement in live events, create designated "Black spatial hubs" and lasting relationships for disparate fan communities.

This framework is precisely why Verzuz filled the void for established Black musicians (Legacy artists and OGs) to maximize and re-engage audiences through digital tools. In a digital event that resembled the traditional rollout of a festival tour. For participating artists, Verzuz presented a unique opportunity to perform from the comforts of their own homes, bantering with one another and giving the backstories to the biggest songs in their catalogs. The concept of stage presence is so different in an in-person brick and mortar venue versus on a livestream. Daniel Glogower, a vice president of Timbaland's music tech startup BeatClub explained:

> Verzuz is actually demanding a new type of performance from big-name musicians. Because you have the audience there but they're reacting in a very different way. You don't hear the applause. You can't see their faces most of the time. So you have to think of other ways to engage them and also for yourself to feed off of their energy in a way that isn't' immediate applause. Acknowledgment of the comment section is a prime example of how we have seen Verzuz evolve to become a more immersive experience. Also the amount of impressions on social media days after has steadily increased. (Personal Communication, November 23, 2020)

It would appear that affordances granted to Verzuz artists is not a temporary fix but the start of a new normal: a live music experience that truly blends online and offline elements. Writing on extended liveness in television, Ytreberg (2009) argued that the broadcast media industry exploits live audience participation via digital return channels for the purposes of revenue, competitive edge, and strategic expansion. In regards to the music industry, this new situation has similar implications on the interplay between live music events, social media, and online use of recorded music. Since festival attendees in the physical world both consume and produce their concert experiences (Morey et al., 2016, p. 251) on social media, video sharing, and livestreaming platforms, meanings and identities of festivals and their attendees are amplified and extended through such activities. For that reason, there are now commercial aspects of the online extensions of Verzuz as a digitally mediated festival (event merchandise, special edition album bundles and digital VIP experiences) that are coming to fruition and that these aspects will change the way Hip-Hop and R&B artists monetize live music forever. Since metrics of audience participation have also become important to the mystique of livestreaming events, audience members are adding value to the event in both economic and social terms. As a by-product, the status of each audience member and their contributions to the celebration are made salient (Robinson, 2015).

Verzuz is a great example of how the use of mobile phones has become essential to monetizing the "extended" experience of music fandom. In Bennett's (2014) study of the fan community of Tori Amos, she examined texting and tweeting and other forms of mobile phone use at live events that are directed toward a fan audience that is not physically present. In exploring what is gained or lost in the incorporation of online social platforms into the live experience, Bennett concluded that media engagement often disrupts the "flow" experience of the fans who are physically present, while at the same time delivering a great amount of pleasure to those who are not present. Kjus and Danielsen (2014) expressed similar arguments regarding mobile phone use, arguing that socially distant audiences better use their mobile devices to prepare and process, document and communicate the event on online platforms before, during and after it.

In thinking about how all of this relates to the popularity of Verzuz, the inability of fan audiences to attend live events during 2020s pandemic has only served to intensify and extend the impact of Verzuz events in the attention economy. The amount of user-generated data on social media created before, during, and after each live webcast has been record-breaking and sets a new precedent for legacy artists to showcase their music catalogs in front of hundreds of thousands of people simultaneously. As Jayson,* a veteran Entertainment lawyer explained to me:

> If big name artists want to do livestreaming long term and grow that audience I think there's not as big a barrier to it. They can do that by being super consistent about it, not just putting on one acoustic set and calling it a day. Really being consistent about it and actually reaching out to other artists who are also live streaming. Similar to how in podcasting so much marketing and promotion happens organically among talent guests appearing on each others' shows. (Personal Communication, December 28, 2020)

In less than a year, *Verzuz* has become a premier virtual concert series—one with its own lexicon and community—that has the ability to both revive and spark new audiences for Black legacy artists who take its virtual stage. Fans, music executives, and celebrities all participate equally, and though *Verzuz* participants only play ninety-second clips of their songs, metrics indicate that viewers are more engaged than they would be after a live concert. Ultimately, that remarkable engagement has major implications for artists vying for viewers and listeners in the new stay-at-home world.

THE VERZUZ EFFECT?—MONETIZING BLACK NOSTALGIA THROUGH LIVESTREAMING

Since 2017, Hip-Hop has emerged as the overwhelming favorite as the most listened to genre in the global music industry (Rys, 2017). Surprisingly, Verzuz has allowed Hip-Hop stars from these prior generations to re-emerge bigger than before, as new artists to those younger members in the Hip-Hop generation and igniting the collective memories of older fans to revisit their catalogs via streaming services. Over twenty million people have watched Verzuz performances on Instagram since they started in March 2020 (Shaw, 2020) and that is a testament to the power of Hip-Hop. To this point, Dave Mays, Founder of Hip-Hop magazine *The Source* explained:

> One thing that I want you to take into consideration, is that Hip-Hop culture has emerged as the winners during this pandemic. Verzuz is just another example of how Hip-Hop always is at the forefront of innovation no matter what is going on in the world. When shit goes wrong in the world, Hip-Hop always finds a way to continue thriving. In this case, Hip-Hop's OGs tapped into social media and used it in a way that no other music genre has managed to. Verzuz allows us to connect to the history of the culture and celebrate it. With that, comes people looking to profit from it. (Personal Communication, November 15, 2020)

One thing that Mays elucidates here is the idea that the artist narratives and collective memories of the audience are what makes Verzuz so immersive and dynamic. Teresa Gowan (2002) noted extensively of the ways that individuals frame their present everyday lives through the lens of nostalgia. In defining nostalgia, she leaned on Kathleen Stewart's (1988) work which suggested that nostalgia can look different between those that have a certain amount of agency (possession) over their lives and those that lost a significant amount of agency over the course of their adulthood (the dispossessed). Gowan's (2002) work also found that collective memory played an important role in how her subjects gained comfort through a communal experience of catharsis. When conversing with many men who lived on the streets, she found they often would not only mention their visits to bars as a source of camaraderie but also something that they felt they deserved because of the stressors (family and professional) that they endured in their everyday lives.

In similar fashion, one could argue that a lack of agency in everyone's everyday lives during the COVID-19 pandemic and the civil unrest in United States (surrounding the murders of Ahmaud Arbery, Breonna Taylor and George Floyd) left few options for Black people looking to happily unite as a community, reclaim their racial pride and engage with the outside world but also to reclaim a positive connection to their heritage. Given that void,

Verzuz emerged, allowing the catalogs of Black music megastars from prior generations to ignite the collective memories of fans to revisit their catalogs via streaming services, attend the battles on Instagram, hold discourse about their performances and publicly share their personal connections to the music of the respective artist-participants. C-King*, a very well-known New York City-bred Hip-Hop artist, explained how nostalgia played a big part in his attraction to attending the Verzuz battles:

> Perfect example, when I was listening to the RZA and Premier battle, I wasn't keeping score cards like my boys. I was just going off how I felt because I've judged so many beat battles. And In that moment, it's really how that beat, what they played made you feel. Not how it played against the other song. OK he played Liquid Swords, he played So Ghetto. I'm not judging them against the songs. I'm judging how they each made me feel in the moment and the moment that I first heard those records. (Personal Communication, December 8, 2020)

Because the music being played during Verzuz battles holds a certain quality and weight for audiences that is extremely nostalgic, people who attend the battles are listening to the music and on-stage dialogue much differently than if they attended a live concert. Likewise, Verzuz battles are also educational for the young people who are tuning in that may not have been a part of the eras from which the artists' work first emerged. But how do artist's make revenue in this environment? Harrison*, a popular Chicago Hip-Hop radio station disc jockey explained to me why he felt legacy artists were best positioned to monetize their brands and grow their fan base through Verzuz:

> Clearly, the ways in which Verzuz has helped artists win is through streaming and just the sheer amount of brand awareness brought about in this time of national quarantine. Typically, the streaming game has been one that was forward thinking with new cultural production. But in this market, having a legacy catalog that is from the CD era and being under-utilized by streaming services is the surest bet in this climate. Verzuz is blowing artists up who haven't been relevant in a decade or more or play major roles behind the scenes as songwriters and producers . . . That is genius. (Personal Communication, December 8, 2020)

Hip-Hop and R&B Musicians have typically not had genre-specific pathways for reviving collective memory and cultivating intimate relationships with their consumers that didn't include a significant amount of travel for promotion. For that reason, Verzuz has become one of the most influential shows for boosting these artists' streaming numbers, leading to higher increases than the likes of more ubiquitous marketers like late night network talk shows and popular music programs like NPR's Tiny Desk Concert. One respondent who works as a content manager at Apple Music told me:

> Verzuz artists' streaming numbers jump by 88% in the three days following the show compared to the previous three days. Artists who performed on The Late Show with Stephen Colbert only see their streams go up by on average by 5%. Verzuz has helped artist streaming numbers after performances more than Saturday Night Live, Live with Jimmy Fallon and NPR's Tiny Desk Concert series. That's huge. (Personal Communication, December 10, 2020)

Billboard magazine reported comprehensively on the streaming numbers that Verzuz artists receive in the three days following the events (Cochrane, 2020). They reported that during producer/songwriters Kenneth "Babyface" Edmonds and Teddy Riley's *Verzuz* battle, the combined forty-nine tracks played by the two artists rose a total of 115 percent in on-demand streams, with 1990s hits like Tevin Campbell's song "Can We Talk" and Blackstreet's "No Diggity" garnering well over 100,000 plays each. Additionally, Jill Scott and Eykah Badu's collective streaming numbers tripled in the days following their battle, and both Beenie Man and Bounty Killer reached their highest single-day streams of 2020 on the day after their battle. Similarly, the matchup showcasing Gladys Knight and Patti Labelle drew in over 3.7 million views across Instagram and Apple Music, and it helped both LaBelle and Knight more than triple their streams. In the three days following the show, Knight saw a 252 percent increase in on-demand audio streams, while LaBelle saw a 219 percent lift, compared to the previous three days. Lastly, the battle between R&B singers Brandy and Monica drew in six million viewers between Instagram and Apple Music and rose both of their catalogs' streaming numbers over 200 percent in the same timeframe (Lavin, 2020). Apple Music's Head of Content, Larry Jackson said to Rolling Stone, "In the eight years I've been in the business of music streaming, it is the best idea that I've ever seen or heard for catalog. The exponential growth of these artists who participate in these battles... the only other thing I've seen that has been this good for catalog is the Super Bowl halftime show" (Millman, 2020, p. 2).

Beyond the gains in streaming, *Verzuz* gives legacy artists who've largely receded from the center of pop music a spotlight moment—often their first in some time—and gives them clout as social media influencers. Babyface's Instagram followers jumped from 300,000 to 1 million following his battle with Riley, DJ Premier nearly doubled his Instagram followers after battling RZA, and Ludacris had over 200,000 social media posts made about him during the three hours of his battle with Nelly. In November 2020, Rappers Gucci Mane and Jeezy's Verzuz battle was watched by a record-breaking 9 million people and generated 7 billion social media impressions.

As a virtual event, the staggering ability of these events to hold the attention of masses of people (without screen fatigue) is largely due to the extended ability for audience members to share nostalgic stories and memories audiences have over these artists and their biggest hits. As Mark M. told me:

> The commentary surrounding these events can guide how we shape our collective tastes in music much better than an algorithm can. And that's the way in which often those (artists') stories can re-enter our psyches in such a powerful way for the course of a week or two. And (music) always needs a gatekeeper I think to be able to present that type of power. Verzuz is serving as that collective gatekeeper for our legends to enter this new virtual model of connection.

Since its infancy, Verzuz has created new pathways for analog musicians to contribute to the global digital landscape in ways that reorient attention from genre-blurring amateurs. Unlike Napster in the 1990s, Myspace in the early 2000s or the 2010s where YouTube first emerged, Verzuz appears to be a business model for the 2020s that shifts the economic pathways of musical artists. In using social media to engage, resist, negotiate, and evade copyright law and typical record label constraints, Verzuz artists and audience members are using digital practices to reclaim nostalgia on new terms. As ICM Partners veteran booking agent Mitch Blackman told Rolling Stone magazine, "This isn't just a live concert anymore. It's something else, it's going to be a whole field. A whole 'nother music industry" (Millman, 2020, p. 2).

CONCLUSION

Verzuz as a Black Technoculture, Relational Labor, and the New Live Music Model

In this chapter, I have theorized about Verzuz as innovating the future of live music by analyzing Verzuz audience members as active commentators, songs as interventions, and their social media profiles as sites of resistance in the face of economic crisis and the elimination of in-person audience connection. Currently, being loved (or heavily engaged with) on social media is just as important to the career development of a R & B or Hip-Hop artist as any song they can create. Verzuz is creating micromoments that fans can organize around and provide them a similarly robust currency as they would gain from a live in-person festival concert.

However, the formula to sustaining this currency during a time of social lockdown is still much of a mystery. In the context of live music, the COVID-19 outbreak has been framed primarily as an economic crisis, in which the music-based products and practices through which revenue is derived have been abruptly and, arguably, irreparably disrupted by a global public health emergency. However, Verzuz's emergence in the wake of this crisis may only ever be a catalyst to what may be an upheaval in the structure of the live music experience itself. In order to develop and advocate for effective economic solutions which meet the longer-term needs of touring recording artists, it is important to understand the challenges created by fundamental changes to the ways public spaces can be occupied, and to consider how the music industry might meaningfully adapt.

Even so, the disruption of the established spaces of music practices also heralds a potential time of change and new directions, with Verzuz potentially representing the seeds of a blended on/offline live music offering and a recalibration of control within the music industry. I believe the social arena for Verzuz and its various labor practices originates in the "Clout Economy"—a technosocial system in the marketplace of attention built around African Americans resisting constraint and socially hacking online spaces for cultural capital and sustained celebrity that can be monetized. In an ecosystem where cultural production is characterized by its flow both online and offline and relentless pursuit of "digital clout," technosocial currency of influence and power is recognized through the accumulation of a loyal and engaged online audience. It is important to note that Verzuz started with no direct commercial objective but instead was user-generated and disseminated through ordinary channels for online communication (social media) and now, music listening (streaming services), as well as production channels operated by the professional apparatus (major record companies and their label affiliates) are monetizing the media activity surrounding the event.

Unfairly compensated by the record companies and digital music service providers, many recording artists have long shifted their focus toward concert tours as their primary source of income. As DIY social media-driven global campaigns behind Verzuz have demonstrated, these preexisting structures and spaces of the music industry are no longer fit for purpose in the time of COVID-19. Though interviewees suggest that likely that a return to "business as usual" post-COVID-19 may not be possible, they also see Verzuz as cause for optimism that grass will be greener on the other side. The advancement of digital innovations such as artificial intelligence, virtual reality, livestreaming technology, and social media have transformed the live music industry into a "live-concert-streaming music industry" Verzuz is an example of how the spatial crises (venue closures and capacity constraints) in the music industry during the COVID-19 lockdown do not have to be inextricably linked to a narrative of economic crisis but rather one for which new economic opportunities have emerged.

REFERENCES

Aguilar, M. (Host). (2020a). How the hell will artists make $ going forward after this with Cherie Hu (No. 111) [Audio podcast episode]. In *Think Like A Rapper Podcast*. Kidz in the Hall LLC. Retrieved from https://https://podcasts.apple.com/us/podcast/111-how-hell-will-artists-make-$-going-forward-after/id1450210761?i=1000473137496

Aguilar, M. (Host). (2020b). IG live is raps only fans & rethinking movie promo in the tiger king age with Jerry L Barrow. (No. 109) [Audio podcast episode]. In *Think Like A Rapper Podcast*. Kidz in the Hall LLC. Retrieved from https://podcasts.apple.com/us/podcast/109-ig-live-is-raps-only-fans-rethinking-movie-promo/id1450210761?i=1000471703475

Anderson, C. (2007). *The Long Tail: How Endless Choice is Creating Unlimited Demand*. New York, NY: Random House.

Baym, N. K. (2013). Data not seen: The uses and shortcomings of social media metrics. *First Monday, 18*(10), 1–7.

Baym, N. K. (2018). *Playing to the Crowd: Musicians, Audiences, and the Intimate Work of Connection*. New York, NY: NYU Press.

Bennett, L. (2016). Fandom, liveness and technology at tori Amos music concerts: Examining the movement of meaning within social media use. In Reason, M., & Lindelof, A. M. (Eds.), *Experiencing Liveness in Contemporary Performance: Interdisciplinary Perspectives* (pp. 64–75). New York, NY: Taylor & Francis.

Brock Jr, A. (2020). *Distributed Blackness: African American Cybercultures*. New York, NY: NYU Press.

Brown, S. C., & Knox, D. (2017). Why go to pop concerts? The motivations behind live music attendance. *Musicae Scientiae, 21*(3), 233–249.

Cochrane, N. (2020, September). The Verzuz effect—Why Apple is betting big on battles. *Billboard*. Retrieved from https://www.billboard.com/articles/news/cover-story/9430242/verzuz-effect-swizz-beatz-timbaland-instagram

Danielsen, A., & Kjus, Y. (2019). The mediated festival: Live music as a trigger of streaming and social media engagement. *Convergence, 25*(4), 714–734.

Duffy, B. E., & Hund, E. (2015). "Having it all" on social media: Entrepreneurial femininity and self-branding among fashion bloggers. *Social Media + Society, 1*(2), 2056305115604337.

Evans, J. M. (2020, May 24–28). We (MOSTLY) carry guns for the internet: Online visibility, relational labor and chasing digital clout in Chicago's drill rap scene [Conference presentation]. 2020 Annual International Communication Association Conference, Gold Coast, Australia. Retrieved from https://ica20.vfairs.com

Florini, A. (2020) *Beyond Hashtags: Racial Politics and Black Digital Networks*. New York, NY: NYU Press.

Gowan, T. (2002). The nexus: Homelessness and incarceration in two American cities. *Ethnography, 3*(4), 500–534.

Holt, F. (2010). The economy of live music in the digital age. *European Journal of Cultural Studies, 13*(2), 243–261.

Jenkins, H. (2006). *Convergence Culture*. New York, NY: NYU Press.

Kjus, Y., & Danielsen, A. (2014). Live islands in the seas of recordings: The music experience of visitors at the Oya Festival. *Popular Music and Society, 37*(5), 660–679.

Lavin, W. (2020, September). Brandy and Monica earned over 20 million combined streams after 'VERZUZ' battle: The pair's battle broke the record for simultaneous viewers in the series thus far. *NME*. Retrieved from https://www.nme.com/en_asia/news/music/brandy-and-monica-earn-over-20-million-music-streams-after-verzuz-battle-2746300

Maaso, A. (2018). Music streaming, festivals, and the eventization of music. *Popular Music and Society, 41*(2), 154–175.

Marwick, A. E. (2013). *Status Update: Celebrity, Publicity, and Branding in the Social Media Age*. Yale University Press.

Millman, E. (2020, September). 'Verzuz' is giving an unparalleled boost to artists. *Rolling Stone*. Retrieved from https://www.rollingstone.com/pro/news/pandemic-verzuz-streaming-growth-1065198/

Morey, Y., Bengry-Howell, A., Griffin, C., Szmigin, I., & Riley, S. (2016). Festivals 2.0: Consuming, producing and participating in the extended festival experience. In J. Taylor (Eds.), *The Festivalization of Culture* (p. 251–268). London, UK: Routledge Publishing.

Naveed, K., Watanabe, C., & Neittaanmäki, P. (2017). Co-evolution between streaming and live music leads a way to the sustainable growth of the music industry–Lessons from the US experiences. *Technology in Society, 50*, 1–19.

Robinson, R. (2015). *Music Festivals and the Politics of Participation*. Farnham, UK: Ashgate Publishing, Ltd.

Rys, D. (2018, January 5, 2018). 2018 Preview: With business booming, new pressures on the music industry. *Billboard*. Retrieved from http://www.billboard.com/articles/columns/Hip-Hop/7669109/mixtapes-moneyHip-Hop-shadow-economy-mainstream

Shaw, L. (2020). Swizz and Timbaland. *Bloomberg Business, 135*(17), 20–21

Stewart, K. (1988). Nostalgia—a polemic. *Cultural Anthropology, 3*(3), 227–241.

Taylor, I. A., Raine, S., & Hamilton, C. (2020). COVID-19 and the UK Live Music Industry: A Crisis of Spatial Materiality. *The Journal of Media Art Study and Theory, 1*(2), 219–241.

Watkins, C. S. (2019). *Don't Knock the Hustle: Young Creatives, Tech Ingenuity, and the Making of a New Innovation Economy*. Beacon Press.

Wikström, P. (2009). The adaptive behavior of music firms: A music industry feedback model. *Journal of Media Business Studies, 6*(2), 67–96.

Ytreberg, E. (2009). Extended liveness and eventfulness in multi-platform reality formats. *New Media & Society, 11*(4), 467–485.

Chapter 7

Black and Quarantined

Celebrating Black Identity during COVID-19 via Instagram

Katrina Overby, Gheni Platenburg, and Niya Pickett Miller

On Sunday, September 13, 2020, 3.7 million viewers tuned in across the platforms Instagram and Apple Music to watch the highly advertised and anticipated Verzuz battle between R&B legends Patti LaBelle and Gladys Knight (Gunn, 2020). As expected, the iconic ladies were dressed to the nines as they sat center stage in cushioned white chairs beneath chandelier lights in Philadelphia's historic Fillmore Theater. For the next two hours, the two longtime friends and singers embarked on a musical and story-filled journey down memory lane, bringing viewers along for the nostalgic ride.

Variety reporter A. D. Amorosi (2020) described the highly anticipated event featuring the ladies' top hits as a "lovefest" and "a cross between a mutual-admiration society, a church service and a good talking-to from your mother" (para. 1). Viewers of all ages tuned in from multiple digital spaces to listen, comment and sing along to the songs that served as the soundtrack to the viewers' lives. Billboard writer Andrew Unterberger (2020) stated, "It didn't even seem like anyone watching in the comments or on social media was bothering to play favorites or keep score between them," (para. 55).

Following the ending of the competition, of which there was no clear winner, said Unterberger, audiences moved to what is best described as the after-party at Club Quarantine. The virtual venue was hosted on legendary DJ Derek "D-Nice" Jones' Instagram (IG) Live. For the next few hours, viewers could enjoy some of the perks of a traditional club experience—good music, fellowship with other club-goers—along with the perks of partying from home—unlimited food and drinks of viewers' choosing, relaxed, come as you are attire, and comfortable and available seating. The night was just one of several examples that emerged during 2020 of Black people coming together online to bond over a shared love of music, converse about life and musical opinions and enjoy each other's company. As the world struggled to quarantine for periods during the COVID-19 pandemic, Black people have found comfort in visiting virtual community spaces like Club Quarantine and Verzuz.

As communication and media scholars who are actively engaged participants in contemporary and popular Black cultural moments, we lean on our positionalities as young Black womxn in the academy to explore our experiences observing and participating in Club Quarantine and Verzuz. Utilizing these lenses, we draw from cultural frames of reference to explicate the intersections of race, class, communication, and culture in this chapter. Thus, through watching, listening, discussing, and preserving, we examine the significance and process of Black connectivity through Club Quarantine and Verzuz during the ongoing pandemic.

As social media usage during the COVID-19 pandemic increased, viewership of Club Quarantine and Verzuz also soared. Each of the Verzuz battles have consistently broken livestreaming records. For instance, the Verzuz battle between Atlanta-based rappers Young Jeezy and Gucci Maine surpassed records on Instagram and Twitter. The @verzuztv Instagram page reported that 9.1 million people tuned in to watch the battle. However, there were a number of Black-owned restaurants and bars that hosted watch parties to create an in-person live-viewing experience together, as did individual clusters of family and friends. Thus, the actual amount of viewers that tuned in may be much larger than what has currently been reported.

Club Quarantine proved to be equally as popular. As of January 15, 2021, D-Nice's Instagram page boasted 2.5 million followers, a large swell from 1.2 million followers in late March (Broaddus, 2020). There is no formal count of the Club's viewership since March 2020, but the number of attendees has averaged to over 150,000 depending on the day and time.

Sharing information, creating, and preserving communities has become increasingly important during the nationwide shelter-in-place order. As Americans grapple with understanding the medical implications of the Coronavirus and the government's response to the pandemic, many also wrestle with the mandated challenge of social distancing. States have taken various actions including implementing safer at home mandates (Edwards, 2020), closing nonessential businesses, restricting venue capacities (Texas Department of State Health Services, 2020), and even enforcing curfews.

In the beginning months of the pandemic in 2020, Black and other marginalized communities were skeptical and discontent with the Trump administration's rhetoric and mishandling of communities of color as the virus further exacerbated the disparities in healthcare among marginalized groups. In a May 2020 *Politico* article, reporter Laura Barron-Lopez (2020) wrote:

> Basic tenets of communicating to the public during a pandemic—like articulating empathy and maintaining consistent messaging from government officials—have been ignored by the Trump administration during the coronavirus outbreak, dozens of public health professionals have told *Politico* in recent weeks. The effect of those missteps has been exacerbated in minority communities that were already distrustful due to long-running racial inequities in the health care system, they said. (Barron-Lopez, 2020, para. 7)

Quarantining—imposed isolation to mitigate contagion—has become the socially responsible action that everyone can do in response to the pandemic. However, the practice of social distancing challenges our inherent need for identification with others. Therefore, escape from the harsh realities of COVID-19 has expanded the need for virtual community and social connection.

Accordingly, people have turned to "digital leisure spaces" on the Internet (Silk et al., 2016). Schultz and McKeown (2018) defined digital leisure as "time spent engaged in digital practices and spaces while in a leisurely state of mind" (p. 223). Social media platforms provide space and opportunity for entertainment, information, escapism, and social and political engagement. Instagram (IG), in particular, has increased its position as an information hub and Black digital leisure space during this time, earning the nickname of "music's best concert venue" (Frank, 2020, para. 5).

Our exploration of how Instagram functions as a multigenerational digital leisure space while rhetorically sustaining American Black culture, identity, and community during the COVID-19 pandemic via Club Quarantine and Verzuz is significant for a few reasons. First, Instagram's livestreaming function allows for the chronicling of the Black lived experience in real time. Second, Club Quarantine and Verzuz are examples of the evolution of Black community building via social media. Finally, this exploration presents an opportunity to further explore the untold stories of the Black community during a challenging social climate—politically, racially, and physically and mentally. With these justifications in mind, we seek to better understand the ways in which Black cultural exchange has been creatively reimagined and sustained during a global pandemic via Club Quarantine and Verzuz on the social media platform Instagram. Next, we present a brief history of how both livestreaming events were created to provide context for our discussion.

WELCOME TO THE PARTY: BLACK DIGITAL BLOCK PARTIES VIA CLUB QUARANTINE AND VERZUZ

Club Quarantine and the Verzuz battles have become the quintessential place to go and *be* Black while in quarantine. Although these livestreamed events are obviously digital, logging on the event as a viewer often feels as if you are attending mentally, emotionally, and physically with others. These experiences are culturally analogous to the Black "a cookout" or "club vibe." Speaking on DJ D-Nice's Club Quarantine, *Chicago Tribune* columnist Kevin Williams said, "For me, the D-Nice set brings to mind the phrase, 'It's a black thing, you wouldn't understand'" (Williams, 2020, para. 2).

Club Quarantine

The phenomenon that is now Club Quarantine began on Thursday, March 17, 2020, with D-Nice using his Instagram account to do a simple livestream of himself deejaying from Los Angeles in his home's kitchen. He only attracted about 200 guests, but word of the virtual event began to spread. Two days later, D-Nice held a nine-hour jam session playing everything from classic R & B and hip-hop to Afrobeat and pop music. Each passing hour brought more attendees, eventually topping 100,000 (Ju, 2020).

Attendees included Black celebrities of all ages and professions such as Naomi Campbell, T.I., Usher, Lionel Richie, Patti LaBelle, Gladys Knight, Lenny Kravitz, Gayle King, Oprah, and even Michelle Obama. Some non-Black guests even showed up like Joe Biden, Bernie Sanders, and eventually Mark Zuckerberg, the owner of Instagram and Facebook. What also made the event special was the interactivity between all those involved. D-Nice not only played music but he also responded to the conversations in the livestream's comment sections. Guests like Lenny Kravitz sent the DJ drinks via delivery. Guests also conversed with each other about the event in the stream's comment section and on other social media platforms. For instance, Jelani Cobb, of *The New Yorker*, described the event as "part dance party, part social-media therapy, and a health-policy initiative cleverer than anything the government has put together" (Cobb, 2020, para. 2).

By the end of the night, D-Nice had secured a place for himself in pandemic history with what was dubbed as Club Quarantine. "I never would've imagined that the best party I would create and DJ would be from the comfort of my own home. Homeschool is a thing! Yesterday was absolutely insane. The amount of artists and friends that virtually partied with me far exceeded my expectations. I'm feeling nothing but gratitude. Thanks to all of you that supported. This has been a great way to keep our spirits high,"

D-Nice (2020) wrote in a heartfelt Instagram post following the initial success of the event (para. 1).

Since then, he has regularly hosted Club Quarantine. His sets range anywhere from one hour to a few hours. He also does not keep a set schedule. Sometimes he parties with a specific purpose such as promoting voter registration (Thornton, 2020). Other times, he starts a session whenever the mood strikes day or night.

Even after stay-at-home mandates loosened, both celebrity and noncelebrity guests have continued to attend. In a March 23 Instagram post, D-Nice wrote, "I had a tearful moment this morning after realizing that we all came together as a global community and danced while I played music in my living room. It was beautiful to experience and I'm truly humbled by the amount of love I've received. Thank you to everyone that supported me on this journey. Let's continue to uplift each other as we get thru this dark time" (para. 1).

Verzuz

The Verzuz battles initially began as a DJ battle between mega producers Swizz Beatz and Timbaland in March 2020. The live webcast series quickly became popular among Black Instagram viewers during the initial nationwide mandates and curfews for quarantining. As the need to be in community with one another while simultaneously being entertained, Black viewers' anticipation of the battles increased.

As the Verzuz battles proved to be extremely successful over the course of the first couple of months, garnering millions of views and reactions during their livestreamed Instagram broadcasts, they received the attention of several entertainment companies. Thus, through the support and partnership with digital media giants, the Verzuz battles production value was increased. With heightened production quality, artists began to showcase more and more creativity. These are illustrated through such moments as Gucci Maine and Jeezy competing in the same venue with king-like thrones at the famous and notable Atlanta strip-club Magic City to guest appearances from legendary artists such as Dionne Warrick who stopped by and sang with Patti Labelle and Gladys Knight during their monumental battle.

The selected opponents for the celebrity match-ups in the Verzuz battles are rooted in communal nostalgia and long-standing fan rivalries and debate that have existed for decades. The battles somewhat allow for a cultural resolution as to which artist created the best music and which dj/producer is the best in a particular genre. Understanding the significance of the match-ups requires cultural competency, appreciation, and knowledge of the genre coupled with the familiarity of the extensive music catalog of both artists.

The Verzuz battles have become not only the place for the Black community to gather virtually but also in-person as several restaurants and bars have hosted viewing parties similar to boxing matches as newer mandates have allowed for indoor dining and social gatherings. Additionally, many of the artists who participate in the Verzuz battles have proven to benefit from what the hosts are calling the #VerzuzEffect. That is the significant uptick in social media imprint (followers, YouTube views, music streams, etc.). This allows us to witness the importance of race and culture in the digital sphere and its need for further exploration.

While a number of theoretical frameworks can be employed to explain the community interest and success of Club Quarantine and Verzuz, we focus on just two—Black identity and Black digital media usage. As we grapple with better understanding the communicative identity practices of Black folx in the social media sphere, these two frameworks provide the best lens in which to consider patterns that emerged from exploring Club Quarantine and Verzuz.

BLACK IDENTITY, DIGITAL LEISURE SPACES, AND COMMUNITY BUILDING

The root of attraction for these digital venues stems in large part from this shared Black racial identity. Janet Helms (1990) generally defined racial identity as, a collective identity based on one's perception that he or she shares a common racial heritage with a particular racial group. People have a natural tendency to socially migrate toward people who share similar traits to ourselves.

Think back to school lunchtime. For the most part, we made seating decisions based on where we felt most accepted and be ourselves. The reasons all the Black kids sat together in the cafeteria are the same reasons why Black people now flock to shared digital spaces—a shared racial heritage and a perceived safe space to openly celebrate, observe, and discuss Blackness (Tatum, 1997). As technology plays an increasingly important role in our lives, researchers have begun taking a closer look at technology's relationship with race and other human dimensions (O'Byrne & Hale, 2018).

During Club Quarantine and the Babyface versus Riley challenge, Instagram users expressed their enjoyment and cultural connection by posting streams of dance, praise-hands, power fist, music notes, wine glass/cocktail, and heart emojis. The emojis coupled with text phrases such as: "Let it breathe," "Yasss or Yazz," and partial song lyrics (of the music playing) filled the comment section of the screen and provided an immersive Black cultural social exchange. Such exchange is *identification*, a key element needed for human persuasion and connectivity. As Burke (1950) explains, identification is the process of joining interests. He expounds:

> A is not identical with his colleague, B. But insofar as their interests are joined, A is identified with B. Or, he may identify himself with B even when their interests are not joined, if he assumes that they are. (pp. 20–21)

To apply Burke's thoughts, individuals in the Black community will identify with others *exhibiting* similar interests. They also identify with others whose interests are *perceived* as similar to their own, or when someone else *demonstrates* that they are similar. This helps to explain how and why Instagram's Black-themed livestreaming events have proven to be an effective space for Black community engagement and digital leisure during this pandemic.

Both Club Quarantine and the Verzuz battles offer a space for Black visual and vernacular identification. Through these digital events, accepted ideological codes that reify Black positivity narratives and culture are vetted for identification and then consubstantiated, because we have questioned our ability to live inside the rhetoric offered online and find solace within specific Instagram spaces. Black social interaction is an important element to creating and sustaining Black cultural identity. Shared communal experiences and moments reinforce the importance of engagement for Blacks, often finding ways to revolutionize and reinvent spaces for community.

Social media have provided such opportunities for online community building and alternate publics (Steele, 2018) for marginalized communities that may otherwise not exist. In order to examine the ways in which identity work and community building has been mediated through Instagram for Blacks during the pandemic, it is important to discuss the technological affordances of Instagram that makes this level of connection possible.

CTDA and IG's Technological Affordances

This chapter draws from Andre Brock's Critical Technocultural Discourse Analysis (CTDA) as a critical approach and framework through which this rhetorical exploration of the Club Quarantine and Verzuz livestreamed events can be achieved. Brock (2020) discussed how to use CTDA to evaluate digital artifacts and practices, specifically Black online cyberculture. CTDA requires that you read information technology as text, it accounts for cultural identity expressions and takes the "contributions of Blackness to digital practice" (p. 23) into consideration. To expound on the importance of exploring Black cultural online identity, Brock (2020) argued:

> Networks, bandwidth, interfaces, hardware, and environment mediate social performances of online identity, but how racial identity affects those social

performances is understudied. The effects are bidirectional; an examination of cultural online performance must incorporate both the intended and unintended audience's technologically and culturally mediated reception of that performance. This has not always been the case in internet and new media research. (p. 20)

Yet, as the affordances of live Instagram streams don't allow for an archiving of information between viewers and participants, we explore how to examine these interactions despite these constraints. To this end, analyzing livestreamed events is understudied and worthy of examination as Black cultural performance takes place in many forms on social media platforms.

Steele (2018) used CTDA to analyze the affordances and constraints of blogs to cultivate alternate publics for African Americans online. Similarly, in this case, we utilize CTDA to explore the affordances and constraints of IG's livestreaming function (from an individual's own account) to mediate engagement and participation for collective moments of cultural celebration and expression. As previous research about Black cyberculture and discourse has primarily focused on examining Black Twitter, we explore the use of IG's livestreaming function by Black folx during the COVID-19 pandemic to expand what is currently understood about Black cyberculture and Black identification practices during a modern crisis. Based on our observations as participants and scholars, we discovered similar patterns of Black community, identity, and communication building between Club Quarantine and Verzuz that will be explained through what we denote as the 3 Cs: Celebrity, Communication, and Community.

In This Together: *Celebrity* Engagement and Influence

During the pandemic, government leaders and medical professionals have sought to deliver a number of public health messages to the masses in a worldwide attempt to minimize the spread of COVID-19. To increase message dissemination, they rely on a long-utilized strategy of enlisting people with influence to be their message conduits. Community leaders (Pitts, 2020), social media influencers (Ravindranath, 2021), and celebrities volunteered, and in some cases, were recruited (Intarasuwan, 2020; Gardner, 2020) to encourage others to stay home, quarantine, wear masks, wash hands, get vaccine shots, and even help "boost confidence in President Donald Trump's response to the pandemic" (Diamond, 2020, para. 2). Black celebrities also joined these efforts individually and collectively, wielding their influence as opinion leaders in the Black community (Buckley, 2021).

One of the most memorable moments happened on March 30, 2020, as revered actor and producer Samuel L. Jackson read the comical yet serious-toned poem *Stay the Fuck at Home* from a book on *Jimmy Kimmel Live*, and it was shared on several social media platforms. Author Adam Mansback remixed his original poem *Go the Fuck to Sleep*, which Jackson had previously read for an audiobook. The opening lines read:

> Stay the fuck at home. Corona is spreading, this shit is no joke. It's no time to work or roam. The way you can fight it is simple my friends, stay the fuck at home. Now technically I'm not a doctor. But motherfuckers listen when I read a poem. So here I am, Sam Fucking Jackson, imploring you: Keep your ass at home. If you want things to get back to normal, don't panic. Just use your dome. Wash your hands, stop touching your face and stay the fuck at home. (Jimmy Kimmel Live, 2020, 6:10)

In this same essence as Samuel L. Jackson, D-Nice, Swizz Beatz, and Timbaland created platforms that not only became information hubs but also sustainable spaces for the enjoyment of Black music and culture that allowed Black folx to join in by simply using their mobile devices, computers or televisions while staying at home. In support of these movements, a number of Black celebrities actively participated in both Club Quarantine and Verzuz seemingly to encourage their respective fan bases to find ways to stay entertained during quarantine.

Celebrity participation is integral to maintaining the hype during the Verzuz battles, as they engage in organic commentary about the competitions by interacting with each other and fans in the comments. This has created a new public-facing connectivity for fans to witness, observing their favorite artists and celebrities engage with one another during the battles in real time. The majority of the comments that appear in viewers' live feeds are from Black celebrities, in which some comedians have grown to be key commentators who provide witty and relevant humor both before and after the battles. One of whom is the self-appointed scorekeeper comedian Tony Baker (Instagram page @tonybaker), who comments after every song to give a score for that round and hosts a postbattle Instagram live chat with his fans. While comedian Anthony Adams, known as Spice Adams (Instagram page @spiceadams), is best known for his parodies that are quickly posted after some of the battles. For example, he masterfully reenacted the Teddy Riley vs. Baby Face battle where legendary R&B artist Teddy Riley attempted to be extra with a live band and encountered a number of sound and technical issues, causing the hosts to reschedule the battle at a later date.

Meanwhile, Club Quarantine also positioned itself as a place for both celebrities and noncelebrities to intermingle online. As the virus progressed, people found themselves grounded at home and looking for entertainment and social interaction. Seeing celebrities like singers Chaka Khan and Alicia

Keys, rappers and producers like Ludacris and DJ Khaled and actresses like Tracee Ellis Ross and Kerry Washington partake in the sets helped cement the reality that the pandemic was affecting everyone regardless of profession, age, or income bracket. The presence of celebrities at Club Quarantine also helped disseminate the safer at home mantra that has dominated the pandemic.

In many ways, Club Quarantine mimicked the traditional day party or nightclub experience, including celebrity engagement. D-Nice showed love to his influential visitors through shout-outs as they trickled into his sets and added their comments to the live feed. Part of the broadcasts' charm is the elimination of the VIP sections of the traditional physical party setting. At Club Quarantine, there is no division based on finances, clout, or prominence. Everyone parties together in the same room with the same music. This model provides space and time for celebrities to interact with their fans and vice versa. On August 29, 2020, Instagram user @NMarchdev wrote that she had a fun time at Club Quarantine and thought it was "pretty cool" that she saw rapper Fat Joe there (Archeval, 2020, para. 1).

Additionally, D-Nice also uses his sets to praise the work and impact of musical celebrities. Some of his sets focused on specific musical icons. For example, on August 20, 2020, D-Nice performed a Mariah Carey themed set titled, "CQ: The Butterfly Effect." From her home, Carey even appeared alongside D-Nice in a separate livestream window to provide commentary. Carey praised D-Nice's work. "You have saved the day." "You have become such a part of everyone's healing during this moment" (D-Nice, 2020, para.1).

Finally, Black political leaders were invited to these platforms to encourage voter engagement and mobilization during election season. One of the most notable appearances was from politician and voting rights activist Stacey Abrams who addressed viewers prior to the showdown between Atlanta-based rappers Gucci Mane versus Young Jeezy Verzuz battle. In her remarks, Abrams attempted to emboldened viewers to be civically engaged and to vote in the January Georgia senate race to flip the state blue. Moreover, Abrams applauded the community service efforts of the Atlanta based rappers, insisting that they were very important to their fans and the city of Atlanta at large.

Club Quarantine also provided a platform for political guests and discussions. D-Nice regularly partnered with organizations pushing voter registration and voting. For example, in October 2020, D-Nice partnered with the nonprofit group When We All Vote and former first lady Michelle Obama to host #CouchParty to encourage people to get out and vote for the 2020 presidential election.

In addition to the actual sets, D-Nice mobilized his entire Instagram page to push for political change. Guests coming to his page for Club Quarantine would encounter posts pushing political advocacy. He thanked Stacey

Abrams for her work in winning the Democratic votes in Georgia, celebrated Joe Biden's presidential win and even served as the deejay for Biden's first speech after he was officially declared the winner of the 2020 Presidential Election.

The Art of Black *Communication* Practices in Da Virtual Club

Collective cultural communication practices are a key aspect that marks these spaces as Black during Club Quarantine and Verzuz. Congruent with other previous research on Black digital communication practices, viewers utilize variations of collective communication practices in their interactions on social media with each other. Black racial identity that is performed online through several rhetorical and oral traditions, like signifyin' and storytelling, mark the spaces as Black. The use of Black vernacular and signifyin' practices are mapped onto the unfiltered commentary among many viewers resulting in culturally relevant, oftentimes humorous, and intellectually witty Black online identity performance. Brock (2020) explained, "Where once people relied on memory and anecdotal experience to fix individual identity in time and space, the internet provides an endless archive of identity performance—or as Black online culture calls it, 'receipts'" (p. 19). As such, we individually screen captured and archived several comments from the livestreamed events that illustrate the notion of identity performance during Club Quarantine and Verzuz.

As Black vernacular and signifyin' communication practices are an important aspect of participating in the exchanges of commentary during the Club Quarantine and Verzuz live streams, culture and context become equally significant to enjoying and participating in these events. Viewers of both events, including celebrities, actively communicate shared community sentiments through vibes, which can be understood as mood-inducing and behavior influencing song lyrics/beats, language, and atmosphere.

As a primary example, Club Quarantine's communication practices are evident through both expressed sentiments made by D-Nice and attendees and the song lyrics of the music played. Throughout the series' D-Nice regularly shares his mantra of "good vibes," a call to action for shared positive energy among attendees. The music D-Nice plays during his sets is purposeful and intentional.

While some sets are played to create a high-energy party mood, other sets are curated with love songs or decade, genre, artist, or topic-specific music. For example, on Jan.1, 2021, D-Nice curated a "recovery vibes" set of R&B and soul music to help listeners recuperate from the previous night's New Year's celebration by playing a selection of smooth grooves (D-Nice, 2021, para. 1). From his DJ cubby complete with mood-lighting, his playlist included songs from Dennis Edwards, Rose Royce, Hall & Oates, and Faith Evans. Additionally, for his fiftieth birthday on June 20, 2020, he played a set of some of his favorite grown people music songs that ran the gamut of John Legend's "So Gone" by John Legend to Odyssey's "Native New Yorker" and C-Murder's "Down for my N's."

Scholars have continually proven the unifying, restorative, and mood-impacting nature of music (McClean, Bunt & Daykin, 2012; Barron, 2013; Bicknell, 2009). One example of this came from Club Quarantine attendee Maribel Gamboa. Gamboa, otherwise known as @Nyazbos_lady, shared on Instagram that her husband was recovering from multiple brain surgeries over the last few months. She credited D-Nice's Club Quarantine with helping his recovery.

In a November 11, 2020, Instagram post, she shared a photo of herself and her husband in his hospital room relaxing and listening to D-Nice play The O'Jays "Stairway to Heaven" during Club Quarantine (Gamboa, 2020, para. 1). She captioned the post "#Thankful for saved sets that continue to carry us through the dark times and #connect us in all celebration of life and #unity Thank you, @Dnice" (Gamboa, 2020, para. 1). Another example came in a September 7, 2020, post from Renee Ortega, otherwise known as @movewithrenee. Ortega shared a video of herself happily dancing in her living room to D-Nice's Caribbean set on Labor Day. She captioned her post, "When you think your [sic] done for the day but @Dnice hits those #EasternParkway hits & it's party on. #laborday2020 (Ortega, 2020, para. 1).

Additionally, during a New Edition set on September 11, 2020, participants showed their appreciation to D-Nice for the nostalgic music. A Boston native, Instagram user @Natti213 called the set "everything," while another user @Ceearia wrote that she was "smiling through this entire set" (D-Nice, 2020, para. 1).

We Are One: The Value of Black Community in Digital Spaces

Black people share a sense of community forged through their racial connection. Verzuz and Club Quarantine offered a communal space for Black people to temporarily escape the stress and chaos of the real world and celebrate the music that has been the soundtrack of Black history. The creators of both Verzuz and Club Quarantine have been very clear on their intentions for their spaces to be concert equivalents of the metaphorical cookout. For instance, D-Nice has continually expressed his desire to spread good vibes to his viewers.

The mythical lure of the Black cookout came to life during these virtual livestreamed events and have equally been reminiscent of a Friday or

Saturday night out at a concert or club for many viewers. The consistent amount of people tuned in for these events, that have reached tens of thousands of viewers, indicate Black community members' need to be connected with one another in one place at the same time. Furthermore, the viewership is exemplar of the generational diversity in the Black community. As the cookout has always included individuals from every generation in the family, Club Quarantine and Verzuz provided something for everyone in each generation. This has helped solidify the value placed on unity and culture in the Black community.

Case in point, the Patti Labelle versus Gladys Knight Verzuz battle brought together several generations of viewers, some who weren't initially familiar with these legendary artists' extensive catalogs. In a sense, Verzuz has played a pivotal role in sustaining the longgevity of some of the community's most important musical figures and legends across generations. Each battle provides another opportunity for viewers to encounter the work of artists who have made significant contributions in their genres.

Viewers are instrumental to creating a unifying sense of community during Club Quarantine and Verzuz. During the Verzuz battles, the artists sang or rap along with their song tracks during the battles, which created a concert-like experience. In these moments, it has become practice for viewers to engage with each other by typing their favorite song lyrics and flood the livestream with emoticons and stories about how they connect with the song. Furthermore, viewers enhanced the experience by simulating the interactions and conversations that would take place if they were enjoying the battles in-person. Viewers prepare and plan for these battles as if they were attending live concerts.

Similar to a usual concert going experience, they coordinate activities with each other prior to, during, and after the event. As is true with other aspects of Black cultural engagement, there is crossover between Club Quarantine and Verzuz as viewers from the Verzuz battles share that they are headed over to hear DJ D-Nice after the event. Meanwhile, Club Quarantine was born out of a mission to bring people together.

Whether it was for a holiday celebration or just a Tuesday after work, the online club experience provided a reason and opportunity for people to enjoy music together in the same space at the same time. For Halloween, D-Nice prompted his audience to hang out together online when he dressed up as horror movie figure Jason and played a themed set. By the time many people were sick of being shut-in for the virus in late December, D-Nice once again encouraged his audience to join him at Club Quarantine for a New Year's Eve party.

Throughout the club's run, D-Nice has regularly vocalized that his goal was simply to spread love to others. In an April 2, 2020, post he wrote "This is not an escape—this is a reminder of what love can be . . . This is why I play music on IG Live. Spread love" (D-Nice, 2020, para. 1). D-Nice also emphasized community by addressing matters of social injustice and political disenfranchisement on his Instagram page, which is an extension of the actual Club Quarantine sets. During the 2021 Presidential Inauguration, D-Nice proudly served as the official.

Presidential Inaugural Committee's "We Are One" event—celebrating the Black community.

Additionally, he often made posts shining a light on the systematic killing of Black men and women at the hands of law enforcement.

IT'S A CELEBRATION: APPRECIATING AND EMBRACING BLACK CULTURE

Black spaces in the digital sphere are an important element to Black identity engagement and community building. Brock (2020) argued, "The internet's interactivity and archival capacities provide interesting spaces within which to articulate identity. In these areas, digital text and multimedia—information—become the meaning-making substrates from which we understand individuals and groups" (p. 19). Thus, it is a necessity to continue exploring these digital spaces as they evolve.

Although a shared racial heritage does not lead to a monolithic approach to life, it has been repeatedly proven that there are indeed shared similarities in ideologies, and interests among people of the African diaspora. Specifically for African Americans, a shared sense of dancing, music, and clothing, and in this case club etiquette, all collaborate to create the Black culture on display in the Verzuz battles and Club Quarantine jam sessions. To understand Black culture is to understand Black performance.

Collectively enjoying music and artist battles are ways Black folx celebrate and acknowledge who we consider to be great in the music entertainment industry. Yet, it is important to note that Black people are eclectic within their own cultural preferences, in this case music. Black people enjoy and appreciate several forms/genres of Black music. Verzuz and Club Quarantine are both examples of the FUBU—for us by us—approach to community work.

The creators of both saw a need within the Black community to not only encourage people to stay home but to also provide entertainment for them. During the pandemic, Black people have grappled with a bevy of emotions stemming from the heaviness of the ongoing health, social, and economic crises underway. For many people, Verzuz and Club Quarantine have played important roles in surviving these challenging times.

As Black people tuned into Club Quarantine and Verzuz to celebrate their culture, identity and love for Black music, they also tuned in to collectively heal. The Sunday, May 31 Verzuz battle between award-winning gospel artists Kirk Franklin and Fred Hammond was appropriately labeled "The Healing." While being at the crux of racial unrest as a result of police brutality and the rising COVID-19 death toll, the iconic artists gathered to essentially give hope to the hopeless, wearing Black and White "I Can't Breathe" shirts to challenge injustices in the police system. What has become one of the most memorable Verzuz battles to date was an evening of uplift and restoration for viewers.

Creating safe spaces for Black folx to be their authentic selves, whether digitally or nondigitally, can seem to be an almost impossible task. Yet, we are able to observe the need and desire for these spaces through our exploration of Club Quarantine and Verzuz. We strongly believe that these will continue to be digital spaces that provide entertainment and solace for Black viewers in the after years of the pandemic.

REFERENCES

Allegra, F. (2020, April 8). How "quarantine concerts" are keeping live music alive as venues remain closed. *Vox*. Retrieved from https://www.vox.com/culture/2020/4/8/21188670/coronavirus-quarantine-virtual-concerts-livestream-instagram

Amorosi, A. D. (2020, September 14). Gladys Knight and Patti LaBelle Turn Sunday's Verzuz "Battle" Into a Lovefest. *Variety*. Retrieved from https://variety.com/2020/music/news/gladys-knight-patti-labelle-verzuz-1234769382/

Archeval, N. [nmarchdev]. (2020, August 29). Instagram. Retrieved from https://www.instagram.com/p/CEfzO8tnfOD/

Barron, B. L. (2013). Ballads behind bars: The music of Lyfe Jennings as art, critique, and healing remedy. *Callaloo, 36*(2), 403–413.

Barron-Lopez, L. (2020, April 21). Trump coronavirus response feeds distrust in black and Latino communities. *Politico*. Retrieved from https://www.politico.com/news/2020/04/21/race-coronavirus-outreach-197470

Bicknell, J. (2009). *Why Music Moves Us*. Palgrave Macmillan.

Buckley, C. (2021, January 28). Tyler Perry gets Covid-19 vaccine on TV to reassure black skeptics. *The New York Times*. Retrieved from https://www.nytimes.com/2021/01/28/arts/tyler-perry-covid-vaccine-skeptics.html

Broaddus, A. (2020, March 24). DJ D-NICE's Instagram live party tops 160K, brings out A-list celebrities. *KARE-TV*. Retrieved from https://www.kare11.com/article/news/health/coronavirus/dj-d-nices-instagram-live-party-tops-160k-brings-out-a-list-celebrities/89-9a555293-3455-4d2f-9403-aad422b93a54

Brock, A. (2020). *Distributed Blackness: African American Cybercultures*. New York, NY: New York University Press.

Burke, K. (1950). *A Rhetoric of Motives*. New York, NY: Prentice-Hall.

Cobb, J. (2020, March 22). D-Nice's Club quarantine is what you need. *The New Yorker*. Retrieved from https://www.newyorker.com/culture/culture-desk/d-nices-club-quarantine-is-what-you-need

D-Nice [Dnice]. (2020, March 1–2021, January 31). Official Instagram for D-Nice. Retrieved from https://www.instagram.com/dnice/

Daniel-Tatum, B. (1997). *Why Are All the Black Kids Sitting Together in the Cafeteria?* New York: Basic Books.

Diamond, D. (2020, September 29). HHS ad blitz sputters as celebrities back away. *Politico*. Retrieved from https://www.politico.com/news/2020/09/29/hhs-ad-blitz-sputters-as-celebrities-back-away-423274

Edwards, J. B. (2020, April 30). Stay at home order, office of the Governor. Retrieved from https://gov.louisiana.gov/home/

Frank, A. (2020, April 8). How "quarantine concerts" are keeping live music alive as venues remain closed. *Vox*. Retrieved from https://www.vox.com/culture/2020/4/8/21188670/coronavirus-quarantine-virtual-concerts-livestream-instagram

Gardner, C. (2020, April 22). "They've made it personal": How California is enlisting star residents for stay-at-home PSAs. *Hollywood Reporter*. Retrieved from https://www.hollywoodreporter.com/rambling-reporter/theyve-made-it-personal-how-caliFornia-is-enlisting-star-residents-stay-at-home-psas-1291231

Gunn, T. (2020, September 22). Patti LaBelle and Gladys Knight broke personal streaming records after Verzuz battle. *Revolt*. Retrieved from https://www.revolt.tv/news/2020/9/22/21451546/gladys-knight-patti-labelle-streaming-verzuz#:~:text=Verzuz%20reported%20that%20the%20epic,impressions%20across%20social%20media%20outlets.

Helms, J. (1990). *Black and White Racial Identity: Theory, Research and Practice*. Westport: Praeger.

Houghton, E. S. (2020, April 6). How D-Nice united a socially isolated world with club quarantine. *GQ*. Retrieved from https://www.gq.com/story/d-nice-interview-2020

Intarasuwan, K. (2020, March 25, 2020). NY, NJ recruit celebrities to urge residents to stay home, donate to coronavirus relief fund. *NBC New York*. Retrieved from https://www.nbcnewyork.com/entertainment/entertainment-news/new-york-new-jersey-recruit-celebrities-to-urge-residents-to-stay-home-donate-to-relief-fund/2342995/

Jimmy Kimmel Live. (2020, April 1). Samuel L. Jackson Says Stay the F**k at Home [Video]. *YouTube*. Retrieved from https://www.youtube.com/watch?v=sSrbxyna4z4

Ju, S. (2020, March 28). How DJ D-Nice's club quarantine became an isolation sensation. *Variety*. Retrieved from https://variety.com/2020/music/news/dj-d-nice-club-quarantine-rihanna-michelle-obama-interview-1203541666/

McClean, S., Bunt, L., & Daykin, N. (2012). The healing and spiritual properties of music therapy at a cancer care center. *The Journal of Alternative and Complementary Medicine, 18*(4), 402–407.

Gamboa, M. [@Nyazbos_lady]. (2020, November 11). Official Instagram for Lizzo. Retrieved from https://www.instagram.com/p/CHcM1PKn8yS/?igshid=lcld7vpej7jv

O'Byrne, I., & Jon Hale (2018). Employing digital spaces to resist harmful discourses: intersections of learning, technology, and politics showing up in the lowcountry. *Learning, Media and Technology, 43*(4), 390–399. DOI: 10.1080/17439884.2018.1498351

Ortega, M. [@movewithrenee] (2020, September 7). Instagram. Retrieved from https://www.instagram.com/p/CE21SAUAjNP/

Pitts, J. (2020, April 16). Baltimore NAACP sound truck circulates "stay-at-home" health message at spots where people are still gathering. *Baltimore Sun*. Retrieved from https://www.baltimoresun.com/coronavirus/bs-naacp-covid-truck-20200416 -mpps6wnqanfu5pxlrviihivcry-story.html

Ravindranath, M. (2021, January 30). Social media "micro-influencers" join effort to get America vaccinated. *Politico*. Retrieved from https://www.politico.com/news/ 2021/01/30/vaccine-rollout-influencers-463917

Schultz, C. S., & McKeown, J. K. L. (2018). Introduction to the special issue: Toward "digital leisure studies." *Leisure Sciences, 40*(4), 223–238.

Silk, M., Millington, B., Rich, E., & Bush, A. (2016). (Re-)thinking digital leisure. *Leisure Studies*, *35*(6), 712–723.

Steele, C. K. (2018). Black bloggers and their varied publics: The everyday politics of black discourse online. *Television & New Media, 19*(2), 112–127. DOI: 10.1177/1527476417709535

Steele, C. K. (2016). The digital barbershop: Blogs and online oral culture within the African American community. *Social Media + Society, 2*(4). DOI: 10.1177/2056305116683205

Texas Department of State Health Services (2020, October 13). Checklist for wedding venues. Retrieved from https://www.dshs.texas.gov/coronavirus/docs/opentx /Wedding-Venues.pdf

Thornton, C. (2020, March 25). Michelle Obama and DJ D-Nice to host "couch party" voter registration live on Instagram. *Black Enterprise*. Retrieved from https ://www.blackenterprise.com/michelle-obama-and-dj-d-nice-to-host-couch-party -voter-registration-live-on-instagram/

Unterberger, A. (2020, September 13). LaBelle in "Verzuz" battle of soul legends: See Billboard's scorecard for the event. *Billboard*. Retrieved from https://www.bil lboard.com/articles/columns/pop/9448297/gladys-knight-patti-labelle-verzuz-battl e-scorecard/

Williams, K. (2020, March 25). DJ D-Nice has just the thing for your coronavirus isolation blues, in a viral dance party. Don't miss shows coming up from Roy Kinsey, Ratboys, Tijuana Hercules. *Chicago Tribune*. Retrieved from https://www.chicagot ribune.com/entertainment/music/ct-ent-d-nice-club-quarantine-coronavirus-dance -party-0325-20200325-ev57duoj6vavngavcdxhtfzuge-story.html

Chapter 8

The Culture Wins

Continuing Black Cultural Traditions through Verzuz

Karl Lyn

> In making their own way out of no way, African Americans have drawn inspiration, strength, and support from various sources—from their families and communities, from a higher power, from the world of ideas, from the past, from other people and places, and from within themselves.
>
> —Michèle Gates Moresi

The above sentiment reflects the ways in which Black people create possibilities to uplift, affirm, and sustain themselves in the face of adversity. This tradition also resonates with the essence of this chapter. With the severe impact of the novel Covid-19 virus as well as the virulent racism that continues to pervade the United States, Black people are grappling with adversity in multiple capacities. However, they also manage to celebrate life, culture, and community despite these hardships. One way in which Black people have uplifted themselves amid these dismal times is through their engagement with Verzuz. Created by music producers Swizz Beatz and Timbaland, Verzuz is a virtual livestream series wherein two popular Black music artists alternate in playing their hit songs from their respective discographies. In the process, these artists share meaningful stories, perform songs, and engage with countless viewers who watch from their smart devices through Instagram or Apple Music. While Verzuz has widely become a notable source of entertainment, its distinction resides in its Afro-cultural function. The central argument of this chapter is that Verzuz serves as a site for which Black people sustain Black cultural traditions through their embodiment of time, rhythm, improvisation, orality, and spirituality. Each of these elements are mediums through which Black artists and viewers articulate their cultural identities, preserve their historical legacies, and ultimately shape Verzuz into a premiere contemporary symbol for Black expressive culture.

In applying a critical methodology that combines thematic analysis with the TRIOS model (time, rhythm, improvisation, orality, and spirituality), this chapter examines the ways in which Verzuz functions as a forum for sustaining Black life and culture. The TRIOS model is a theoretical framework for understanding culturally unique ways in which Black people experience the world and make meaning of their experiences (Jones, 1991). In other words, time, rhythm, improvisation, orality, and spirituality serve as cultural assets through which Black life and culture thrive (McDougal, 2014). Each of these five dimensions of TRIOS will thematically frame this chapter as they are key tenets for understanding Verzuz and its cultural impact. The first theme that is discussed is time. Within this theme, an analysis of Verzuz will show the ways in which participants communicate cultural values as they engage with the past, present, and future through music, and renegotiate time through unpunctuality. Following this theme is rhythm. This section reveals how Verzuz artists employ song, dance, and instrumental technologies in ways that align with traditional forms of Black expression. Next, the theme entitled improvisation highlights how Verzuz participants engage in comedic commentary, freestyling, and political engagement through culturally specific modalities. The following theme is orality, which examines how music artists' conversations and song selections constitute a variety of Black oral traditions such as storytelling, signifying, and call-and-response. The last theme examined is spirituality, which discusses the cultural role of prayer, soul, and gospel music within particular battles. Each of these themes, borrowed from the TRIOS model, illuminates important data for understanding Verzuz as a continuum of Black cultural traditions.

TIME

The construction of time is an element of the human experience regardless of race; however, its significance is dependent on one's personal and cultural subjectivities. Studies on temporality suggest that people from different cultures develop distinct conceptions of time, which reject the view that time is a fixed or universal concept (Levine, 1997; Levine & Norenzayan, 1999). For example, while Europe and North America habitually abide by clock time, it is a common practice in Trinidad to assert the expression "Any time is Trinidad time" to indicate a less rigid way of living (Birth, 1999). Similarly, the intracultural expression "Colored people's time" is conveyed as an inside joke among Black Americans to satirize a Black person's tardiness (Harris & Steineck, 2010), which further emphasizes the cultural subjectivity of time. These idiomatic expressions suggest that the meaning of time varies according to one's beliefs, attitudes, and cultural norms. Additionally, time as it pertains to past, present, and future is reliant on one's identity and societal understandings (Jones, 2003). For instance, many Black Americans have understood that their racial past in American history deeply influences their present conditions and future trajectory (Dagbovie, 2010). Therefore, notions of early, late, past, present, and future are constructions of time that individuals and groups of people develop per their social and cultural worldviews. Recognizing time in this way yields an important entry point into understanding Verzuz as a vehicle through which Black people engage time in culturally significant ways.

Music artists who participate in Verzuz often arrive later than their scheduled time, which is not necessarily a failure of valuing time, but rather a traditional exercise of self-determination. For example, in the battle of "Snoop Dogg vs. DMX," both artists appeared almost an hour after their expected arrival time, then leisurely poured themselves beverages and ate a few refreshments before officially beginning their music rotation. Their delayed and unapologetic entrance exemplifies the way in which both artists reject mainstream America's standards of time and instead subscribe to their own conventions. This assertion of autonomy reflects a larger tradition in which Black people challenge societal expectations of assimilation and respectability. Following the abolition of slavery, Black people resisted "being a slave to the artificial time of the man-made clock" and instead determined time by "being in tune with their emotions, feelings, and the general flow of things" (Smitherman, 2006, p. 21). In this context, Black people exercised their freedom in part by complying with their own sensibilities of time rather than any imposed societal expectations. In a similar fashion, Snoop Dogg and DMX abstain from the timekeeping demands of society by upholding their own sense of time that better suits their sense of self. In so doing, Snoop Dogg and DMX extend a cultural tradition in which Black people determine their own conditions of living and rely on their own intuitiveness to progress through the world.

Moreover, Verzuz artists reconstruct time by reviving the past through nostalgic music and fashion, which evinces traditional forms of cultural preservation. As Verzuz artists typically hold long careers in the music industry, they often invoke memories of the past through their classic songs and display of old fashion trends. As seen in "Nelly vs. Ludacris," both artists not only reignite the early 2000s through playing their hit songs from that time but also through wearing styles of clothing that reflect that period. Ludacris, wearing a large gold chain, throwback basketball jersey, and afro with a pick comb, and Nelly wearing only a sleeveless white undershirt, both represent a cultural shift in time for many Black people. In the early 2000s, many Black men sported afros, flashy chains, ribbed white tank tops, and oversized sports jerseys as part of a larger street fashion and

Hip-Hop cultural aesthetic (Piazza & Notini, 2017). Nelly and Ludacris' self-display of this 2000s Black aesthetic exemplifies their symbolic return in time and a long tradition of Black cultural dress practices. As early as the colonial period, Black people in the United States visibly expressed and retained their cultural pride through clothing styles and bodily adornment (Miller, 2009). Similarly, Nelly and Ludacris' visual embodiment of 2000s Black clothing trends demonstrates the way in which they value and attempt to preserve the Black cultural customs of that time. In this way, Nelly and Ludacris not only embody the Black cultural conventions of the 2000s but also embody the Black historical tradition of clothing as a visual marker of cultural pride and identity.

In addition to reviving the past, some Verzuz participants also engage the future through performing music that emphasizes prospects of freedom, which align with a cultural tradition of forward-looking approaches to liberation. During a time of heightened racial justice activism throughout the United States, Verzuz creators held a special edition battle to honor Juneteenth, a day in which Black people commonly celebrate the end of chattel slavery in the United States (Jefferies, 2004). This special edition featured "John Legend vs. Alicia Keys." Both artists began their battle by singing Bob Marley's "Redemption Song," which tells a story about how one must liberate their mind and progress toward freedom. One lyric reads, "We forward in this generation triumphantly. Emancipate yourself from mental slavery, none but ourselves can free our minds." Through performing this song, Alicia Keys and John Legend impart the song's future-oriented message of moving forward toward liberation. This future-oriented approach to freedom is consistent with a Black activist tradition of "freedom dreams," wherein Black people envision an alternative future in which they are free from the forces of oppression (Kelly, 2002). Specifically, freedom dreams have been one of the ways in which Black people have radically imagined a future beyond their current conditions that would allow for a "new beginning, and a beautiful, peaceful, collective life" (Kelley, 2002, p. 29). Alicia Keys and John Legend's duet resembles the ethos of freedom dreams as they amplify the song's message of freeing one's mind to imagine a future that is unbounded by the limitations of oppression. In this way, both artists reignite the Black cultural tradition of freedom dreams, and subsequently provoke their listeners to also uphold this tradition as the song prompts them to devise their own visions of freedom.

RHYTHM

In addition to time, rhythm is a culturally specific way in which Black people have personally and communally expressed themselves. As Jones suggests, rhythm is a vehicle for creative communication and cultural survival, allowing Black people to assert themselves in their environment through movement, music, dance, sound, and other modes of expression (Jones, 1991). The evolution of rhythm and its function in Black life and culture illuminates a robust relationship between music and identity expression. During enslavement, Black people were denied the use of instruments for fear that they would compose rhythms to communicate with one another and incite rebellion (Crawford, 2001). However, enslaved Black people still created music by turning household items such as kitchen utensils and washboards into instruments, ultimately blending rhythmic patterns in ways that signaled the sounds of community, celebration, mourning, and survival (Crawford, 2001). Additionally, the rhythms that emanated from the Harlem Renaissance illuminated the rich sounds and aesthetics of Black life, culture, music, and style (Wall, 2016). Langston Hughes, for example, captured the rhythm of jazz in much of his early poetry during this period (Huang, 2011). Moreover, Black people's development of rhythm and blues provided an outlet for Black people to convey their deepest emotions and sentiments, and communicate through rhythm what mere words could not convey (McNamee, 2014). Also, dancing to these rhythms were equally pervasive among many Black communities and continues today as a means of articulating one's identity, culture, and rhythmic talents (Jackson, 2001). With an understanding of this context, one can better grasp the ways in which Verzuz artists use rhythm to sustain Black culturally expressive traditions.

Some Verzuz artists display rhythm through their embodiment of sound, which represent cultural nuances of expression. While artists are only expected to play their prerecorded songs, many artists perform their songs live. "Beenie Man vs. Bounty Killer" is a battle in which both Jamaican artists perform live, and in doing so express their cultural and rhythmic sensibilities. Throughout their performance, both artists often deviate from their song lyrics to hum and utter sounds in rhythm to the cadence of their songs and in harmony with one another. This sonic performance is not only rhythmic because of their ability to melodically blend with one another and their music but also because of the ways in which they seamlessly centralize their oral culture within their performance. According to Louis Chude-Sokei (1997), "the mechanics of sound is a Jamaican cultural tradition where authenticity and identity are ritualistically invented. It is the mechanism by which one group in the Black diaspora distinguishes itself from others" (p. 187). With this understanding, Beenie Man and Bounty Killer situate Jamaican sound culture as the foundation for their performance, and therefore articulate the ways in which their cultural identities and traditions are integral to their music and self-expression. Through this Jamaican cultural practice of sound, Beenie Man and Bounty Killer also distinguish themselves within the Black diaspora, which illuminates the heterogeneity of Black cultural traditions that permeate throughout the world. In these ways, Beenie Man and Bounty Killer sustain and amplify Black cultural traditions through centralizing their Jamaican sound culture, and illustrating the ways in which other areas and people of the African diaspora aside from the United States contribute to the global safeguarding of Black cultural traditions.

In addition to sound culture, some Verzuz artists demonstrate rhythm through extending cultural traditions of dance. Ranging from nodding one's head to full choreography, artists often accentuate their music with movement. This rhythmic physicality appears in "E-40 vs. Too Short." While both artists began their battle sitting down, they both quickly rose from their seats to dance to their songs. Throughout their performance, both artists showcased original dance moves, as well as classic dances such as E-40's moonwalk rendition. Their dances reveal the ways in which they function rhythmically in response to their music. E-40 and Too Short's dancing also aligns with a tradition of Black expressive culture called ritualization. Jackson (2001) states that ritualization refers to "movement, typically dance, that occurs among Black performers and communities in celebration at a ritual event, and involves asserting a pronounced sense of personal style that invites attention from the community" (Jackson, 2001, p. 46). E-40 and Too Short practice ritualization as they are performers who shape their Verzuz battle as a celebratory event wherein they display personal styles of dancing to commemorate one another and their music. They also embody ritualization because of the ways in which they invite attention from the virtual community of viewers who participate in this event as audience members. Therefore, E-40 and Too Short uphold this Black expressive tradition of ritualization as they use dance to communally celebrate one another, engage community, and exhibit their personal sense of style and expression.

In addition, some Verzuz artists manifest rhythm through technological ingenuity by drawing on cultural conventions of Black music production. Specifically, some artists employ DJ practices such as scratching records and changing song tempos to mix and invent new rhythms. In "T-Pain vs. Lil John," both artists use turntables to manipulate the sound, cadence, and style of their songs. As they use their turntables to play their music, they showcase their rhythmic and technological adeptness to digitally customize the flow of their music. T-Pain and Lil John's approach to modifying their music derives from a tradition within Hip-Hop culture wherein Black Disc-Jockeys since the mid-1970s mastered the art of turntablism and declared this practice one of the five elements of Hip-Hop (Rose, 1994). Additionally, Rose maintains that such DJ practices are a form of Black expressive culture because of the ways in which Black musicians have historically customized their music per their creative and artistic talents (Rose, 1994). Thus, T-Pain and Lil John not only extend a key cultural tradition of Hip-Hop through their use of turntables but also a tradition of Black musicality wherein Black musicians demonstrate their ingenuity through restyling their music. As T-Pain and Lil John extend these traditions, they also represent the ways in which Black people have transformed Black cultural customs over time to contend with new and emerging technologies. Thus, T-Pain and Lil John also ensure the survival and accessibility of these cultural traditions by showcasing the ways in which such practices can extend to modern and popular mediums.

IMPROVISATION

Equally important to rhythm is the role of improvisation within Black life and culture. Jones posits improvisation as a creative and individualistic orientation that enables people to manage and adapt to their various circumstances (Jones, 2003). Moreover, Gottschild (1996) argues that "African American culture has always been improvisatory, by force of circumstance with its members adept at code-switching-both in verbal and body language as the need arises" (p. 221). This assertion that improvisation is characteristic of Black culture compliments other literature that suggest that Black people throughout history have illustrated a mastery of improvisation by virtue of their ingenuity and ability to navigate and survive their adversities (Bolden, 2004; Fischlin, 2013; Muyumba, 2009). For example, the masses of Black people throughout the twentieth century who migrated from the South to pursue new possibilities and conditions in the North demonstrated a form of improvisation as they improvised a path for survival in the face of uncertainty and opposition (Grossman, 1989). Other scholars have examined the way in which improvisation was an everyday practice among Black people under slavery (Dusinberre, 2009; Hopkins, 2000; Jones, 2003). Hopkins recounts how enslaved Black people built an "improvised meeting house" for church gatherings by using tree branches and other scarce materials available to them (Hopkins, 2000, p. 107). As it pertains to music, improvisation is a distinct feature of Black music production most popular within jazz music (Muyumba, 2009; Brothers, 1994; Hollerbach, 2004). Black people's improvisational approach to jazz allowed them to "negotiate their identity as an individual, as a member of the collective culture, and as a link in the chain of tradition" (Gilroy, 1993, p. 267). These traditions highlight the ways in which improvisation has characterized Black people's creativity, self-expression, and cultural agency through generations. Likewise, Verzuz serves as a cultural resource wherein Black artists and viewers rely on their improvisational abilities to creatively express themselves in ways that magnify Black cultural legacies.

One way in which Verzuz artists participate in Black improvisational culture is through freestyling. This style of improvisation appears toward the end of "Snoop Dogg vs. DMX" in which both artists freestyle rap to instrumental Hip-Hop beats. During Snoop Dogg's freestyle, he states, "Sit back and enjoy the show, this is the way we flow, off the top it's so original." In this improvised rap bar, Snoop Dogg alludes to his improvisational skills as he emphasizes the originality of his rap, and asserts that his flow is "off the top" which refers to the way in which his words derive from the top of his head in an impromptu manner. Similarly, DMX builds on Snoop Dogg's improvisational performance by freestyling to a different beat about a variety of subjects that cross his mind in the moment. Through these freestyles, both DMX and Snoop Dogg represent a tradition of improvisation distinct to Black music culture. During the Harlem Renaissance of the 1920s, jazz poetry was a popular style of performance in which Black poets such as Langston Hughes experimented with freestyling spoken word to jazz instrumentals (Jones, 2011). Additionally, Black poets of the Black Arts Movement in the 1960s commonly improvised rhymes and poetry throughout their performances (Bracey, Sanchez, Smethurst, 2014). In these ways, Snoop Dogg and DMX extend a cultural tradition wherein Black artists improvise lyrics to jazz instrumentals and perform impromptu poetry. By understanding the ways in which rap is an extension of poetry, one can recognize the ways in which Snoop Dogg and DMX's freestyle raps are rooted in a long legacy of Black artistry and expressive culture.

Additionally, Verzuz audience members evince improvisation through posting spontaneous and comedic comments, drawing on the ways in which Black people historically use humor as a coping mechanism. Verzuz viewers often joke about a range of unexpected moments and observations within a battle, such as the severe technological issues present in "Babyface vs. Teddy Riley." During their battle, Teddy Riley entered the livestream with multiple microphones, speakers, a band, DJ, hype man, and camera crew. Consequently, Teddy Riley experienced a series of technical issues such as distorted sounds, echoed audio, and equipment failure. However, while Teddy Riley and his production team attempted to correct these issues, many viewers began to post jokes in the comments section of the livestream such as "By the time Teddy finally fixes his sound, Babyface will have written and recorded another album" and "Teddy knew he had to find a way to sabotage this battle as soon as Babyface showed up." These comments among many of the others reveal the ways in which viewers identified an unfortunate circumstance, and then improvised an alternative form of entertainment using humor. This practice of turning an unfavorable situation into a comical one reflects a cultural tradition wherein "African Americans developed their distinct form of humor, in which the material of tragedy was converted into comedy, this often included self-deprecation, as the slaves themselves were often the subjects of their comic tales" (Woolfork, 2009, p. 194). In a similar way, Verzuz audience members chose Teddy Riley to be the subject of their jokes, and in doing so transformed this tragic predicament into comedic relief. Therefore, the viewers who improvised their entertainment experience in this way sustain a Black cultural tradition wherein humor is used as a source of social uplift.

Moreover, Verzuz serves as a site for improvisation through the ways in which battles are tailored to the political moment of that time, illustrating a tradition of Black political engagement. While Verzuz is not overtly political, Black politicians have made virtual appearances to prompt viewers to participate in electoral voting. At the beginning of "Jeezy vs. Gucci Mane," Stacey Abrams, former Georgia House Democratic leader and first Black woman to be nominated for Georgian governor, appeared on screen to encourage Georgian viewers to vote in the state Senate's runoff elections. Similarly, vice presidential candidate at the time Kamala Harris (Now first Black woman to become vice president of the United States) made a virtual appearance at the beginning of "Brandy vs. Monica" to commend the music artists for their support of voting initiatives, and ultimately encourage viewers to use their voices by voting in the 2020 presidential election. Since improvisation is a way of "connecting the internal and external world" (Jones, 2003, p. 226), Abrams and Harris' guest appearances are improvisational as they participate in bridging the internal world of Verzuz with the external world of mainstream politics. Abrams and Harris' political outreach within Verzuz reflects a historical tradition of Black leaders who politically mobilized the masses to advocate for Black people's voting rights, citizenship, and political power. Sojourner Truth, Fannie Lou Hamer, Ella Baker, Dr. Martin Luther King are a few of the countless Black civil rights and voting rights crusaders who galvanized Black people around the importance of political participation (Riser, 2010; Pinkney, 2014; Williams & Carson, 1991). From this historical context, Abrams and Harris use Verzuz as a platform to maintain the legacy, goals, and sacrifices of past Black political activists by promoting their ideals to the masses and continuing their tradition of advocacy for political power and participation.

ORALITY

Along with improvisation, oral traditions are a significant way in which Black people transmit their culture, values, and histories. According to Hamlet (2011), "oral traditions refer to the stories, old sayings, songs, proverbs, and other cultural products that have not been written down or recorded. These diverse forms reveal the values and beliefs of African Americans, the things they hold to be true, and lessons about life and how to live it" (p. 27). In this sense, orality serves as a fundamental way in which Black people employ a range of communicative styles to preserve their cultural heritage and impart their values. Moreover, the various forms of orality suggest that Black people are not limited or confined to certain modes of expression, rather relish in their autonomy of self-expression through a myriad of ways. Additionally, Rose (1994) links Black oral traditions to the emergence of Hip-Hop music as she argues that rap acts as a kind of "talking book" that provides Black artists a means of "articulating a specific stance and location within a broader cultural framework" (p. 62). She goes on to say, "rap's orality is a political act—regardless of content—insofar as it functions as a way of enunciating their presence and identity, while destabilizing the status quo" (Rose, 1994, p. 64). Therefore, orality encompasses Black cultural forms of expression wherein Black people individually and collectively communicate meaning, identity, resistance, and culture. In this fashion, Verzuz artists embody orality through relying on Black oral traditions to articulate personal and cultural values.

Many artists who participate in Verzuz engage in Black oral traditions through storytelling. When Verzuz artists play their music, they usually precede or follow their songs with anecdotes regarding their history with the other artist, life experiences in the music industry, and sentiments toward their songs. "Gladys Knight vs. Patti LaBelle" offers a rich and robust illustration of this form of storytelling as they share a plethora of engaging narratives. Throughout their battle, Gladys Knight and Patti LaBelle discussed the love and joy they share for their music and each other. At one point, Gladys Knight tells Patti LaBelle, "I'm a fan of yours, we grew up together, with our dreams and all," She later states, "I hope they get something out of this music we're doing tonight. Because I know you, and I know me, and generally we only do positive things, most of them are love stories, but it's all about life." Gladys Knight's statements tell a story about her and Patti LaBelle's meaningful history of friendship, as well as lessons about love and life. Their conversational storytelling reflects a Black oral tradition wherein storytellers called griots passed down lessons through verbal narrative and song from one generation to the next that "appealed to emotion, provided solace, and fostered a temporary release from chaotic experiences" (Hamlet, 2011, p. 27). Similarly, Gladys Knight and Patti LaBelle's spoken and sung stories impart lessons about love and life, while also supplying musical entertainment that provides a sense of solace from societal chaos. In this way, Gladys Knight and Patti LaBelle emerge as modern-day griots who pass down a range of stories to their listeners through their anecdotal narratives and music. Thus, Gladys Knight and Patti LaBelle not only continue the Black oral tradition of storytelling but also equip their listeners with stories that they can retain and pass down themselves, ultimately expanding the longevity of this oral tradition.

In addition to storytelling, Verzuz artists uphold the Black oral tradition of call-and-response by listening and reacting to one another's music. When an artist plays a song, the other artist often attempts to follow up with another song that matches the subject, mood, or popularity of that song. While many Verzuz battles exemplify this approach, "Jill Scott vs. Erykah Badu" offers a unique example. Erykah Badu began the battle with playing one of her hit songs "You Got Me." In response, Jill Scott followed up with playing her own live version of "You Got Me" since she co-wrote this song with Erykah Badu. This reciprocity through music emanates from the Black oral tradition "call-and-response." Smitherman (1977) suggests that in a call-and-response tradition, "responses function to affirm or agree with the speaker, urge the speaker on, repeat what the speaker has said, or complete the speaker's statement" (p. 104). With this understanding, Erykah Badu serves as the speaker who calls directly to Jill Scott by playing a song that would resonate with her as the co-writer, to which Jill Scott responds by repeating and affirming Erykah Badu by playing her own rendition of the same song. In this call-and-response, Jill Scott and Erykah Badu dialogically signal to one another their regard for each other as co-collaborators, proud contributors, and long-time friends. Thus, these artists exemplify the ways in which they maintain the Black cultural tradition of call-and-response, and ultimately highlight the way in which Black people employ this tradition to actively listen to, acknowledge, and affirm one another.

Furthermore, some Verzuz artists embody orality through amiable trash-talking, which is rooted in Black expressive culture. Verzuz artists typically celebrate one another through kind words and pleasant conversation; however, some artists participate in trash-talking to heighten the fun and humor of a battle. This form of orality is best seen in the first and original Verzuz battle "Swizz Beatz vs. Timbaland." During their music rotation, Swiss Beatz made remarks such as "Tim is getting bodied right now," "He don't want none of this," "ya'll are going to have to check on Tim tonight," to which Tim usually responded with playing a hit song, then putting his hand to his ear to say "Yea I don't hear you talking now," "That's what I thought," "You don't want me to keep going!" These verbal exchanges between Swiss Beatz and Timbaland among the many others demonstrate a Black cultural performance of orality called trash-talk. While trash-talking is societally understood as "insulting or boastful speech intended to demoralize someone" (New Oxford American Dictionary, 2nd Ed., 2005), Swiss Beatz and Timbaland are instead aligned with a Black cultural convention of trash-talk in which such expression is done in a good-natured rather than mean-spirited way. According to Simons (2003), trash-talk is an expression of African American male cultural values and is a natural extension of the African American oral tradition called "signifying" which is a "game-like oral ritual using boastful, humorous, insulting, and provocative comments in an atmosphere of friendly competition" (p. 11). With this understanding, Swiss Beatz and Timbaland participate in the tradition of signifying as they engage in trash-talk to harmlessly amuse one another and foster positive competition grounded in joy, fun, and brotherhood. Thus, Swiss Beatz and Timbaland incorporate this Black oral tradition into their battle, and ultimately showcase the ways in which the origins of Verzuz is steeped in Black cultural customs.

SPIRITUALITY

In addition to orality, spirituality has played a significant role in shaping Black people's lives, culture, and music production. In discussing the historical relationship between spirituality and Black people, Wiggins and Williams (1996) maintain that Black people during slavery found power in spirituals, commonly known as Negro spirituals or freedom songs, as such songs allowed them to define themselves, voice their plight, and express hope (Wiggins & Williams, 1996). These types of spirituals were also sung as protest songs during the civil rights movement to reflect the history of struggle and determination for freedom (Cook & Wiley, 2000). Therefore, spirituals reveal the ways in which Black people musically responded to their bondage and disenfranchisement. Additionally, private and communal prayers have also held significant meaning among Black people as a means through which they could transcend their miseries and attain psychological comfort (Battle, 2006). Praying, along with praising, shouting, and singing, all speak to a spiritually driven culture in which Black people could maintain a sense of self and community (Holmes, 2012). It is also important to note that spirituality for Black people has not always involved religion. Stewart (1999) maintains that Black people have always developed deeply personal spiritual identities that emanate from their inner souls. He further states that this soul force is evident in soul music which emerges from the spirit-filled vitality of the singer rather than any religious motivations (Stewart, 1999). From this context, Black people have embodied spirituality through song, prayer, and soul as mechanisms for personal and communal uplift. This context also serves to better understand the ways in which Verzuz artists sustain Black cultural traditions through spirituality.

Some Verzuz participants embody spirituality through the ways in which they engage in prayer, which illuminates Black spiritual practices of self-preservation and well-being. Following the prevalence of racist police violence and racial justice protests throughout the United States, a special edition of Verzuz entitled, "The Healing," served to provide a sense of comfort and community to viewers. This edition featured "Kirk Franklin vs. Fred Hammond." Both gospel artists played their popular gospel songs and honored the many Black lives lost to state-sanctioned violence. Before Kirk Franklin and Fred Hammond began their performance, influential spiritual leader Bishop T. D. Jakes opened the battle with a prayer in which he states, "Today, we pray for light, because we have seen too much darkness, from Trayvon Martin to George Floyd, we have seen too much darkness." Bishop T. D. Jakes' reference to victims of police brutality, Trayvon Martin (2012) and George Floyd (2020), suggests that the light he prays for is freedom from the darkness that is racist violence. This prayer represents the spiritual tradition of Black people throughout history who have turned to God to cope with and alleviate their oppressive conditions. Throughout the enslavement period and onward, Black people collectively relied on prayer to provide psychological and spiritual solace despite the severity of racism that informed their daily lives (Boyd-Franklin, 1989; Wiggins & Williams, 1996). In this same tradition, Bishop T. D. Jakes engages Verzuz viewers in prayer to collectively find psychological and spiritual solace from the impact of a racist society. Thus, Bishop T. D. Jakes continues a Black spiritual tradition wherein prayer is used as a source of hope and healing amid trying times.

Following Bishop T. D. Jakes' opening prayer, the remainder of "Kirk Franklin vs. Fred Hammond" embodies spirituality through a series of gospel music, which mirrors the Black music tradition of spirituals during enslavement. As Kirk Franklin and Fred Hammond perform their respective songs, they engage their viewers through singing praise and worship songs such as Kirk Franklin's "He Reigns" and Fred Hammond's "No Weapon." The lyrical content of their songs generally deal with humanity, faith, triumph, and perseverance through tribulations. Through these gospel songs, Kirk Franklin and Fred Hammond impart the cultural legacy of Negro spirituals. Jones (1993) maintains that spirituals were "sacred songs created and sung in situations that were deeply meaningful, archetypically human experiences, relevant not only to the specific circumstances of slavery but also to women and men struggling with issues of justice, freedom, and spiritual wholeness in all times and places" (p. 47). Comparably, Kirk Franklin and Fred Hammond's gospel songs not only pertain to the adverse conditions of being Black in America but also serves to provide viewers with a spiritual resource to sustain themselves and protect their well-being through any plight. In this way, Kirk Franklin and Fred Hammond contribute to advancing a cultural tradition wherein Black people use spirituality to sing through their struggles for freedom, and maintain psychological and spiritual wholeness.

Moreover, Verzuz artists embody spirituality through soulful singing, which is rooted in the tradition of the Black church. Some Verzuz artists who perform their songs often sing over their tracks in nuanced and soulful ways.

This style of singing is best seen through "Gladys Knight vs. Patti LaBelle" as they deliver powerful vocal performances throughout their battle. Gladys Knight and Patti LaBelle sung their songs in spirited ways that deepened the intensity and emotion of their songs. Even when their recorded song finished playing, both artists often continued singing as they were moved by the depth of their passion. This type of singing is considered soulful singing, which reflects a spiritual tradition of the Black church. Following the end of chattel slavery, Black people were not welcomed in the churches of white Americans, and therefore built their own churches in which they could freely vocalize their sensibilities in part by singing from their souls (Jackson, 2004). In these churches, Black people sung with "passion and sentimentality that immediately inspired and awakened the soul in themselves and their listeners" (Jackson, 2004, p. 42). Gladys Knight and Patti LaBelle carry out this church tradition of soulful singing as they awaken the soul in themselves and their listeners through their passionate and sentimental performances. Thus, Gladys Knight and Patti LaBelle carry on the soulful singing traditions of the Black church and showcases the way in which Black people continue to use their voices to autonomously express the depths of their personhood.

CONCLUSION

Verzuz and its importance lies in its capacity to provide a space in which Black artists and viewers celebrate and sustain diverse manifestations of Black culture, identity, music, and heritage. In this manner, Verzuz is grounded in the legacies and culture of Black people and engages the wider world from that foundation. As shown through myriad Verzuz battles, Black people engage with time, rhythm, improvisation, orality, and spirituality in ways that vitalize Black cultural and historical ways of living. By using this five-dimensional framework, this chapter renders visible the unique ways in which Black people sustain and centralize their personal and cultural subjectivities. It is with this understanding that one can recognize the ways in which Black people create reservoirs of cultural memory by retaining and extending all that is unique to Black life and culture. Therefore, it is not only the survival of Black cultural traditions that is evident in this chapter but also the unique ways in which Black people actively affirm their own humanity, culture, and identity. Through music, laughter, dance, joy, community, and expressivity, Black Verzuz participants demonstrate their capacity to practice freedom within and outside of resistance. It is in this capacity that Black people can move beyond appeals for acceptance to discover in themselves the power and inner resources necessary to experience self-proclaimed freedom in the larger struggle for liberation. It is through mediums such as Verzuz that empower

Black people to celebrate and revel in the scope and breadth of Blackness in ways profound and necessary. It is also through creating these communal spaces of Black affirmation and celebration that the culture will always win.

REFERENCES

Battle, M. (2006). *The Black Church in America: African American Christian Spirituality*. Malden, MA: Blackwell Publishing.
Beyers, C. (2001). *A History of Free Verse*. University of Arkansas Press.
Birth, K. (1999). *Any Time is Trinidad Time: Social Meanings and Temporal Consciousness*. Gainesville, FL: University Press of Florida.
Bolden, T. (2004). *Afro-Blue: Improvisations in African American Poetry and Culture*. University of Illinois Press.
Boyd-Franklin, N. (1989). *Black Families in Therapy: A Multisystems Approach*. New York: Guilford Press.
Bracey, J. H., Sanchez, S., & Smethurst, J. E. (2014). *SOS—Calling All Black People: A Black Arts Movement Reader*. University of Massachusetts Press.
Brothers, Thomas. (1994). Solo and cycle in African-American Jazz. *The Musical Quarterly*, 78(3), 479–509.
Carson, C. (1991). *The Eyes on the Prize: Civil Rights Reader: Documents, Speeches, and Firsthand Accounts from the Black Freedom Struggle, 1954–1990*. Penguin Books.
Chude-Sokei, L. (1997). The sound of culture: Dread discourse and Jamaican sound systems. In J. K. Adjaye & A. R. Andrews (Eds.), *Language, Rhythm, and Sound: Black Popular Cultures into the Twenty-First Century* (pp. 185–202). University of Pittsburgh Press.
Cook, D. A., & Wiley, C. Y. (2000). Psychotherapy with members of African American churches and spiritual traditions. In S. P. Richards & A. E. Bergin (Eds.), *Handbook of Psychotherapy and Religious Diversity* (pp. 369–396). Washington, DC: American Psychological Association.
Crawford, Richard (2001). *America's Musical Life: A History*. New York: W.W. Norton & Company, Inc.
Dagbovie, P. G. (2010). *African American History Reconsidered*. University of Illinois Press.
Fischlin, D., Heble, A., & Lipsitz, G. (2013). *The Fierce Urgency of Now: Improvisation, Rights, and the Ethics of Cocreation*. Duke University Press.
Gilroy, P. (1993). *The Black Atlantic: Modernity and Double Consciousness*. Harvard University Press.
Gottschild, B. D. (1996). *Digging the Africanist Presence in American Performance: Dance and Other Contexts*. Greenwood Press.
Grossman, J. R. (1989). *Land of Hope: Chicago, Black Southerners, and the Great Migration*. University of Chicago Press.
Hamilton, V. (1985). *The People Could Fly: American Black Folktales*. New York: Knopf.

Hamlet, Janice D. (2011). Word! The African American oral tradition and its rhetorical impact on American popular culture. *Black History Bulletin*, *74*(1), 27–31.

Hollerbach, Peter. (2004). (Re)voicing tradition: Improvising aesthetics and identity on local Jazz scenes. *Popular Music*, *23*(2), 155–171.

Holmes, B. A. (2017). *Joy Unspeakable: Contemplative Practices of the Black Church* (2nd edition). Fortress Press.

Hopkins, D. N. (2000). *Down, Up, and Over: Slave Religion and Black Theology*. Fortress Press.

Huang, Hao. (2011). Enter the blues: Jazz poems by Langston Hughes and Sterling Brown. *Hungarian Journal of English and American Studies*, *17*(1), 9–11.

Jackson, J. D. (2001). Improvisation in African-American vernacular dancing. *Dance Research Journal*, *33*(2), 40–53.

Jeffries, J. L. (2004). Juneteenth, Black Texans and the case of reparations. *Negro Educational Review, The*, *55*(2–3), 107–115.

Jones, A. (1993). *Wade in the Water: The Wisdom of the Spirituals*. Orbis Books.

Jones, J. M. (2003). TRIOS: A psychological theory of the African legacy in American culture. *Journal of Social Issues*, *59*(1), 217–242.

Jones, M. D. (2011). *The Muse is Music: Jazz Poetry from the Harlem Renaissance to Spoken Word*. University of Illinois Press.

Kelley, R. D. G. (2002). *Freedom Dreams: The Black Radical Imagination*. Beacon Press.

Lester, J. (1969). *Black Folktales*. New York: Grove.

McNamee, G. (2014). Blues vs. Rhythm and Blues. *Virginia Quarterly Review*, *90*(1), 222.

Muyumba, W. M. (2009). *The Shadow and the Act: Black Intellectual Practice, Jazz Improvisation, and Philosophical Pragmatism*. University of Chicago Press.

Parker, J. A., Harris, P., & Steineck, R. C. (2010). *Time: Limits and Constraints*. Brill.

Piazza, A., & Notini, S. (2017). *Hip Hop Stylography: Street Style and Culture* (1st English edition). 24 ORE Cultura.

Pinckney, D. (2014). *Blackballed: The Black Vote and US Democracy*. New York Review Books.

Riser, R. V. (2010). *Defying Disfranchisement: Black Voting Rights Activism in the Jim Crow South, 1890–1908*. Louisiana State University Press.

Rose, Tricia. (1994). *Black Noise: Rap Music and Black Culture in Contemporary America*. Hanover, NH: University Press of New England, pp. 62–63.

Simons, H. D. (2003). Race and penalized sports behaviors. *International Review for the Sociology of Sport*, *38*(1), 5–22.

Smitherman, G. (1977). *Talkin and Testifyin: The Language of Black America*. Houghton Mifflin.

Smitherman, G. (2006). *Word from the Mother: Language and African Americans*. Routledge.

Stewart, C., III. (1999). *Black Spirituality and Black Consciousness: Soul Force, Culture and Freedom in the African-American Experience*. Trenton, NJ: Africa World Press.

Wall, C. A. (2016). *The Harlem Renaissance: A Very Short Introduction.* Oxford University Press.

Wiggins, M., & Williams, C. B. (1996). Counseling African Americans: Integrating spirituality in therapy. *Counseling and Values, 41*(1), 16–28.

Woolfork, L. (2009). *Embodying American Slavery in Contemporary Culture.* University of Illinois Press.

Conclusion
Niya Pickett Miller

We have collectively analyzed and discussed how both Verzuz and CQ provide clear articulations of Blackness that spoke (and still speak) to American culture, especially to Black people's existence in America. Verzuz and CQ's initial appeal results from a particular mix of dichotomous circumstances brought on by the COVID-19 pandemic—isolation/connection, innovation/existing technologies, spontaneity/predictability—as well as a deep and abiding love for Black music. Our serendipitous intersection of ideas also demonstrates how social media, particularly Instagram, can be therapeutic, esteem-building, and synchronously link broad audiences across time and distance during crises.

This is the final chapter, which means I should offer conclusive thoughts about all of the scholarly talk offered here. However, it's difficult to wrap up work that is (really) a starting point of sorts. All of the analyses covered in this book focus on the first season of Verzuz and the early (eleven) months of CQ. This is primarily because the authors answered my call for critical inquiry about the communicative significance of CQ and Verzuz. They worked quickly to capture and understand these events in their infancy. My call for contributing authors prompted these diverse scholars to assume their roles as researchers interested in Verzuz and CQ as unique cultural phenomena as they experienced and survived the pandemic—all while knowing these live events were evolving more not yet known. Therefore, I hope to expand what we have started here, and I invite other scholars with similar interests to do the same. No doubt, we have scratched the surface of contextualizing these events as vital Afro-techno and socio moments that functioned as respiratory, celebratory, and memorials for Black musical excellency.

By the time this work reaches production, Verzuz will be well into (if not beyond) its second (and highly anticipated) season on Triller, a video-sharing app, and continued via Instagram. The "battles" are wildly popular and have catapulted sales and streams for its featured artists and accumulated more than five billion impressions (Mitchell, 2021). Capitalizing on their Verzuz success, creators Timbaland and Swizz Beatz became large shareholders in the Triller Network during the first quarter of 2021. Thereafter, the two distributed some of their equity stakes to the forty-six performers who initially appeared on Verzuz. The move made these artists shareholders and partners in Triller Verzuz. This partnership, a significant power move for the artists, changed the trajectory of the music platform and solidified Verzuz as a thematic staple in the (post) COVID-19 entertainment era. Frankly, "there is no more disruptive and innovative brand in music today than Verzuz," said Bobby Sarnevesht, executive chairman and co-owner of Triller (Mitchell, 2021, para. 5). As a result, Verzuz has expanded into sports with planned collaborations with the NFL, NFL Pro Bowl Verzuz, and other sports verticals. Moreover, comedy and other Verzuz-themed live events are planned for the future.

Similarly, D-Nice—byway of Club Quarantine—has enjoyed tremendous success since the pandemic's rise. The DJ has secured major corporate partnerships (i.e., Ford Motor Company) and proved his cross-over appeal through guest appearances for major cultural events such as 2021 The Grammys (official virtual after-party), Super Bowl LV, NBA Allstar party, and Good Morning America's 2021 post-Oscar show. He also DJ-ed the epic Verzuz battle of vintage groups, "The Isley Brothers vs. Earth Wind and Fire," held on April 4, 2021. That mashup was hosted by (one of) The Original King(s) of Comedy and Family Feud host, Steve Harvey, and was the longest Verzuz to date. It lasted more than three hours, demonstrating the intergenerational appeal of (Black) Soul music and the mass appeal of Verzuz with no U.S. mandated quarantines (thanks to an abundance of COVID-19 vaccinations available). In March 2021, D-Nice released new music—a single with R&B singer/song-writer, Neyo and rapper, Kent Jones—signaling the transformative power of his newfound IG celebrity status. Now, while mandatory quarantines are no longer in place, CQ continues to draw large numbers of viewers. Sometimes D-Nice plays music in tribute to an artist's birthday, death, and following a Verzuz battle. Or he jumps on Live (on any given day), with no specified reason simply to create a vibe. It suffices to say CQ is here to stay.

Personally, I hope you enjoyed these works as much as I did editing them. There is much to be gained from analyzing them, as demonstrated. Given the past and continued success of Club Quarantine and Verzuz, it will be interesting to see how both live-streamed music events continue to evolve and remain culturally relevant as the COVID-19 pandemic wanes. We know that Black music shapes and conveys the realities that exist within Black culture and the collective Black experience. This includes Black history, pain, triumphs, and hopes for the future. Whether you are a fan of CQ or Verzuz, or not, it is important to appreciate these livestreamed events as cocreators of American culture, articulations of reimagined Black narratives, and expressions of Black joy in the twenty-first century. Sharing music is a fraction of CQ and Verzuz's remarkableness. Perhaps their more intriguing implications include their ability to dispel notions of rivalry and competitiveness between and within Black music artists and Black music genres, reframe negative tropes of gendered relationships between Black folks, establish intergenerational connections through the rhetoric of music, reinvigorate the value of Black music artistry in the public sphere, and demonstrate (again) the innovativeness of Black cultural expression through technology—all during a global pandemic.

REFERENCES

Mitchell, G. (2021). Triller Network Acquires Verzuz. *Billboard Business* (Online). Retrieved from https://www.billboard.com/articles/business/9536996/triller-acquires-verzuz/

Index

affect, 4, 6, 28, 29, 33–35, 57, 59, 62–64, 67–69
affordances, 65–67
Allaire, Christian, 18
Amorosi, A. D., 95
Anderson, Marian, 42, 43
Ang, I., 68
Arora, P., 60, 66
artist battles, 108
audiences, 20, 25, 33, 35, 42, 45, 46, 59, 62, 66–71, 85, 86, 107
Auntie Dionne, 16
Auntie Gladys, 16
Auntie Patti, 16
authenticity, 5, 16, 25–38, 117

Babyface, 12, 42
Banks, A. J., 2
Barney, D., 63
Barron-Lopez, Laura, 97
Barrow, Jerry L., 82
Baym, N. K., 66–68, 79, 83
Bennett, L., 87
Biden, Joe, 44
Black celebrities, 17, 98, 102, 103
Black cookout, 5
Black cultural traditions, 113–27
Black digital block parties, 98–100; Club Quarantine, 98–99; Verzuz, 99–100

Black digital public sphere, 12–14
Black female artists, 41, 42, 46, 48
Black identity, 95–109; art of Black communication practices, Da Virtual Club, 105–6; Black culture, appreciating and embracing, 108–9; celebrity engagement and influence, 102–5; community building, 100–101; CTDA and IG, technological affordances, 101–2; digital leisure spaces, 100–101; digital spaces, Black community value, 106–8
Black Lives Matter movement, 42
Black people, 7, 43, 44, 47, 96, 108, 113, 115–17, 119, 122, 124–26
Black popular culture, 5, 7, 11
Black sisterhood: and performative healing, 14–15; as solidarity, 14–15
Black women, 5, 6, 10, 11, 13, 14, 16, 20, 42–45, 47, 48, 50–54; artists, 15, 32, 37, 46, 48; friendship, 5, 9, 11, 15; *See also individual entries*
Black women performances, history of, 42–45
"The Boy is Mine," 27–31, 38
Brandy *vs.* Monica, Verzuz battle, 25–38; The Boy is Mine, 27–31
Brock, A., 101, 105, 108
Bureau of Labor Statistics, 61
Burke, K., 101

careers, 11, 16, 27–30, 32, 48, 50, 51, 53, 79, 80
celebrities, 17, 58, 69, 70, 79, 81, 87, 99, 102, 103, 105
celebrity engagement, 102
Chude-Sokei, Louis, 117
clout economy, monetizing, 79–92
Club Quarantine (CQ), 2–7, 57–60, 62–66, 68, 74, 95–98, 100–109, 131–33; Verzuz challenge and, 12
Cole-Bell, Stacy, 44
collective memories, 88, 89
Collins, Patricia Hill, 64
community building, 100–101
competitiveness, 5, 10–12, 25–38, 133
Critical Technocultural Discourse Analysis (CTDA), 73, 101–2
cultural pride, 116
cultural production, 37, 59, 62, 64, 92
cultural subjectivities, 114, 115, 126
cultural tradition, 115–17, 119, 120, 125
culture banditry, 64, 65
cyber ethnography, 66

Danielsen, A., 83, 87
data collection, 71–72
Davis, J. L., 65
Dean, Kasseem "Swizz Beatz." *See* Swizz Beatz
Deuze, M., 59
digital leisure spaces, 7, 97, 100–101
Diva, 27, 28
diva-in-training, 28
DJ's gig, 57–74; affect, 68; affordances, 65–67; audiences, fans, and fandom, 68–71; culture, participating, 63–65; data collection, 71–72; limitations, 73; relational labor, 67–68; shifts, participation online, 71
DMX, 115
D-Nice, 3–4, 6, 57–58, 60, 62, 64, 66, 98–99, 103–8, 132
D-Nice Jones Instagram, 95
Doaks, Celeste, 21

do it yourself (DIY) projects, 2, 92
Duverney, Ava, 19

Edmonds, Kenneth "Babyface," 4
Edwards, Donna, 44
Elliott, Missy, 4
envy, 25–38
Erykah Badu *vs.* Jill Scott, 9–22, 46–48

Facebook, 61–63, 69, 72, 98
fandom, 68–71
fans, 68–71
female-led Verzuz events, 42, 54
festivals, 6, 84, 86
Florini, Sarah, 45
Floyd, George, 125
Ford Motor Company, 60, 132
freedom, 15, 115, 116, 124, 125
freedom dreams, 116

Gates, Henry Louis, 48
Geertz, Clifford, 63
Gibson, J. J., 65
gig economy, 61–63
Gilyard, K., 2
Gladys Knight *vs.* Patti LaBelle, 9–22, 48–50
Goffman, E., 63
Goins, Marnel, 14, 15
Gottschild, B. D., 119
Gowan, Teresa, 88
Graham, Roderick, 13
Great Black Music (GBM), 11

Hamilton, C., 81
Hamlet, Janice D., 121
Harris, Kamala, 44, 52
Harris-Perry, Melissa, 51
Haynes, J., 70
Helmond, A., 62
Helms, Janet, 100
Hesmondhalgh, D., 61, 84
Hip-Hop community, 10, 12, 19, 71
Hip-Hop culture, 57–74

Index

Hobson, Janelle, 43
hooks, bell, 14, 58
Hu, Cherie, 82

improvisation, 7, 113, 114, 119–21, 126
inheritance, 37–38
"It All Belongs to Me," 30

Jackson, J. D., 118
Jackson, Samuel L., 102, 103
Jakes, T. D., 125
Jenkins, H., 59
Jill Scott *vs.* Erykah Badu, 9–22, 46–48
"Jilly from Philly" *vs.* Erykah Badu, 18–21
Jones, A., 125

Kalamu ya Salaam, 11
Kaplan, Josh, 82
Kendall, Mikki, 9
Kernodle, Tammy, 10
Kitwana, B., 71
Kjus, Y., 83, 87

legacy artists, 79–92
live events, 7, 80, 85–87, 131
live music, 33, 34, 81–84, 86, 91, 92; events, 33, 85, 86; experience, 84, 86, 92

Mahon, Maureen, 16
Marshall, L., 70
Martin, Trayvon, 125
Mckenzie, Joi-Marie, 18
McKeown, J. K. L., 97
microcelebrity, 60, 62, 85
Monica *vs.* Brandy, 50–54
Mosely, Timothy "Timbaland." *See* Timbaland
Mühlbach, S., 60, 66
musical togetherness, 2
music industry, 15, 17, 19, 26, 31, 49, 50, 79, 81, 82, 86, 92, 115

music-streaming platforms, 48, 85
My Lord, What a Morning, 43

Neal, Mark Anthony, 16
Never Say Never, 30
Nieborg, D. B., 62

online platforms, 59, 72, 74, 87
Ono, K. A., 48
Oprah Magazine Instagram, 17
orality, 7, 70, 113, 114, 121–24, 126
oral traditions, 105, 114, 121–24
Outley, C., 13

parasociality, 69
participatory culture, 59, 85
participatory online platforms, 59, 64
participatory platforms, 6, 57–74
Patti LaBelle *vs.* Gladys Knight, 9–22, 48–50
performative healing, 14–15
platformization, 62
platforms, 52, 59–62, 64, 65, 70–73, 79, 86
Playing to the Crowd, 67
Poell, T., 62
Pryor, B., 13

Qualtrics, 71

Raine, S., 81
Reagon, Bernice Johnson, 37
relational labor, 6, 59–61, 67–68, 74, 83, 91
rhythm, 116–19
Riley, Teddy, 12
Rogers, R., 64
Rose, T., 65, 122

Schultz, C. S., 97
Senft, T. M., 60, 69, 70
The Signifying Monkey: A Theory of African-American Literary Criticism, 48–50

Simons, H. D., 123
"Sisterhood: Political solidarity between women," 14
Sisters In The Name of Love, 15
Sloop, J. M., 48
Smith, Shawn, 13
Smitherman, G., 10, 123
Snoop Dogg, 115, 120
social media audiences, 34
social media platform Instagram, 97
social media platforms, 2, 6, 18, 62, 73, 79, 97, 98, 102, 103
solidarity, 14–15
spirituality, 7, 10, 52, 113, 114, 124–26
spirituals, 124, 125
Steele, C., 102
stereotypes, 10, 52
Stewart, C. III., 124
Stewart, Kathleen, 88
Swizz Beatz, 10, 18, 22, 26, 27, 32, 41, 103, 113, 132

Taylor, I. A., 81
Timbaland, 4, 9–10, 12, 18, 21–22, 26, 27, 41, 42, 99, 103, 113, 123, 124, 132
Timberlake, Justin, 4
time, 114–16
T-Pain, 118, 119
TRIOS model (time, rhythm, improvisation, orality and spirituality), 114

Unterberger, Andrew, 95

Verzuz, 2–5, 7, 11, 12, 25, 26–27, 41, 80, 86, 88, 89, 91, 92, 96, 97, 100–103, 107, 109, 113, 121, 131–32; audience members, 91, 121; battles, 6, 7, 10, 33, 89, 96, 98–101, 103, 107, 109, 123; Black cultural traditions, 113–27; Black digital public sphere, 12–14; Black nostalgia monetizing, livestreaming, 88–91; Black technoculture, 91–92; Black women and, 41–54; challenges, 5, 9–22; Club Quarantine and, 12; counter public and enclave, 45–54; events, 42, 48, 50, 87; Jill Scott *vs.* Erykah Badu, 9–22, 46–48; mediated Black music festival, 84–87; Monica *vs.* Brandy, 50–54; new live music model, 91–92; Patti LaBelle *vs.* Gladys Knight, 9–22, 48–50; relational labor, 91–92; rhetorical construction, sisterhood, 9–22
virality, 60

Warwick, Dionne, 15, 16
Watkins, C. S., 79
Wiggins, M., 124
Williams, C. B., 124
women, 10–14, 16, 17, 20–22, 25, 31, 36, 37, 44, 52, 53; envy, competitiveness and authenticity, 31–36; in music industry, 31–36; qualitative measures, achievement, 31; quantitative measures, achievement, 31
workers, 61–63

Ytreberg, E., 86

About the Contributors

Mtalika Banda is a PhD Student in the W.E.B Du Bois Department of Afro-American Studies at the University of Massachusetts Amherst. In addition, he is a R.E.A.L Fellow (Research Enhancement and Leadership Fellowship), and a recipient of the W.E.B Du Bois Graduate Fellowship. Through the use of Performance and Autoethnography, Mtali's work explores Black history in the Global African Diaspora. His use of music and narrative help to bridge Black experiences throughout the diaspora, with an emphasis on Malawian history. Mtali is an accomplished jazz saxophonist and composer. Some notable artists he has worked and performed alongside include Sonia Sanchez, Talib Kweli, the Soul Rebels, Charles Neville, and Claudia Acuna. He is also known in the Southern African music scene for his work with Malawian artists such as Masauko, Faith Mussa, and Lawi.

Dr. Janée N. Burkhalter is an associate professor of marketing and the associate dean of Undergraduate Programs in the Erivan K. Haub School of Business at Saint Joseph's University in Philadelphia, Pennsylvania. Dr. Burkhalter teaches and researches at the intersection of entertainment, marketing strategy, and social media. She is a marketing scholar, educator, and strategist with practical experience in marketing communications, career services, entrepreneurship, diversity, and inclusion. Her work has appeared in journals such as *Journal of Advertising, Journal of Marketing Communications,* and *Business Horizons*. She is also coeditor of the book *Maximizing Commerce and Marketing Strategies through Micro-Blogging.*

Kirstin Cheers is a graduate student in communications with an emphasis on critical and cultural studies at the University of Memphis in Memphis, Tennessee. Cheers is a graduate assistant at the Benjamin L. Hooks Institute for

Social Change. She was recently accepted and participated in Yale University's THREAD: Multimedia Storytelling Program in the Summer of 2019. Her work is featured in The Huffington Post, The Root and WeAreMemphis.

Dr. Aisha Damali Lockridge is currently an associate professor of English at Saint Joseph's University in Philadelphia, Pennsylvania. Her research focuses on African American Literature, Black Popular Culture, and Pedagogy. Her monograph, Tipping on a Tightrope: Divas in African American Literature, traces the trajectory of the Diva figure in African American literature. She is currently working on a manuscript on the transformation of the Magical Negress figure in Black literature and popular culture.

Jabari Evans is a PhD candidate in the School of Communication Studies at Northwestern University and a research fellow at the Northwestern Center of Media and Human Development. His research focuses on the subcultures that urban youth and young adults of color develop and inhabit to understand their social environments, emotional development, and professional aspirations. His forthcoming dissertation project, which centers on a Hip-Hop Education program in Chicago Public Schools, has been recognized for awards by the International Communication Association and has been covered by the Chicago Reader, Chicago Tribune, Rolling out Magazine, Ebony Magazine, and Chicago Crain's Business.

Dr. Eletra S. Gilchrist-Petty is professor and chair of the Communication Arts Department at the University of Alabama in Huntsville (UAH). She is the author of three books and more than two dozen other publications. Gilchrist-Petty has held several offices with the National Communication Association (NCA), including chair of the African American Communication and Culture Division and committee memberships on the NCA Teaching and Learning Council, Affirmative Action and Intercaucus Committee, and Legislative Assembly. She is also chair of the Southern States Communication Association's Committee on Diversity, Equity, and Inclusion. Gilchrist-Petty is, furthermore, a past NCA Division winner of the Top Research Journal article and recipient of the UAH Distinguished Teaching Award.

Karl Lyn is a doctoral student in the W.E.B. Du Bois Department of Afro-American Studies at the University of Massachusetts, Amherst. He holds an MEd from the School of Education at the University of Massachusetts, Amherst and a BA in Africana Studies and Educational Studies from Dickinson College. As a literary and cultural analyst, his research lies at the intersection of Black cultural production, narratology, and politics of representation. His current work focuses on the ways in which Black boyhood is constructed within twentieth and twenty-first century literature, and how these representations transcend or reify narrow constructions of Black masculinity. His other research interests include African American educational history, Black political thought, and performance theory within Black popular culture.

June Mia is a PhD candidate of communication at the University of Illinois at Chicago and managing editor at Gender and Society. Her research interests include participatory platforms, policy, and celebrity.

Dr. Katrina Overby is an assistant professor in the School of Communication at the Rochester Institute of Technology. She is an activist scholar who studies Black Twitter, social media and culture, African American cinema, Black feminist media theories, race and popular culture, and scholar activism.

Dr. Niya Pickett Miller is an assistant professor of communication studies in the department of Communication and Media at Samford University where she teaches race and communication themed course. She is an albinism advocate and championed for inclusive communication about people with albinism in her 2019 Birmingham TEDx talk. Her book, *Deconstructing Albinism as the Other* (Lexington Books), critiques the visual tropes of people with albinism in American popular culture. She coauthored, *Lizzo's Black, Female, and Fat Resistance* (Palgrave Macmillan) which examines the self-curated, fat-positive identity and media reactions to an unabashedly proud fat, Black woman. Her scholarship focuses on visual rhetorical criticism of *otherness*, with special interest in popular culture.

Dr. Gheni Platenburg is an assistant professor in the School of Communication and Journalism at Auburn University. She teaches newswriting and multimedia journalism courses. Her research interests fall at the intersection of race and media, with a particular focus on Black identity, media portrayals and social media.

Goyland Williams is a PhD Candidate in the Department of Communication at the University of Massachusetts-Amherst where he is a R.E.A.L Fellow (Research Enhancement and Leadership Fellowship) and a recipient of the W.E.B. Du Bois Graduate Fellowship at the Du Bois Center. Specializing in Rhetoric and Performance Studies, his research is situated in Black studies, social movement rhetoric, Africana critical theory, cultural criticism, and performance theory|(auto)ethnography. Goyland's public facing scholarship and lectures have been featured in *The Art of Voting,* Race Baitr, The Black Teacher Project, SXSW Interactive Festival, and the Health Equity Lab Summit.

www.ingramcontent.com/pod-product-compliance
Lightning Source LLC
Chambersburg PA
CBHW020126010526
44115CB00008B/990